# The HR Healthcheck

*Benchmarking HRM Practice Across the UK and Europe*

**Chris Brewster, Christine Communal, Elaine Farndale, Ariane Hegewisch, Gene Johnson and Jos van Ommeren**

FINANCIAL TIMES
Prentice Hall

Cranfield UNIVERSITY
School of Management

PEARSON EDUCATION LIMITED

Head Office:
Edinburgh Gate
Harlow CM20 2JE
Tel: +44 (0)1279 623623
Fax: +44 (0)1279 431059

London Office:
128 Long Acre
London WC2E 9AN
Tel: +44 (0)20 7447 2000
Fax: +44 (0)20 7240 5771
Website: www.briefingzone.com

First published in Great Britain 2001

© The Centre for European Human Resource Management, Cranfield University, 2001

The right of Chris Brewster, Christine Communal, Elaine Farndale, Ariane Hegewisch,
Gene Johnson and Jos van Ommeren to be identified as authors of this work has
been asserted by them in accordance with the Copyright, Designs, and Patents Act 1988.

ISBN 0 273 65068 8

*British Library Cataloguing in Publication Data*
A CIP catalogue record for this book can be obtained from the British Library.

10 9 8 7 6 5 4 3 2 1

Typeset by Boyd Elliott Typesetting
Printed and bound in Great Britain

*The Publishers' policy is to use paper manufactured from sustainable forests.*

# About the authors

**Chris Brewster** BA (Econ) PhD MCIPD, Professor of International Human Resource Management, joined Cranfield School of Management in January 1985. He has substantial experience in trade unions, government, personnel management and consultancy. In addition to his teaching role, Professor Brewster speaks regularly at international conferences and has acted as a consultant to UK and international organizations, mainly in the areas of personnel policies (the subject of his PhD) and management training. He is the author of several books and numerous articles. He is Director of the School's Centre for Strategic Trade Union Management and Centre for European HRM, conducting comparative research programmes across the world.

**Christine Communal** BA MA PhD, Senior Research Officer, joined Cranfield in October 1998. Prior to her appointment to Cranfield, and in parallel with her PhD, she taught European Comparative Management at the University of Loughborough. She had previously worked in HR in France (for Elf-Atochem) and in Germany (for US WEST International and Pfalzwerke AG). She is a graduate of the Catholic University of Lyon, France (Modern Languages) and the University of Leicester (Management Studies). At Cranfield she plays an active role in the Centre for Research into the Management of Expatriation and in the Centre for European Human Resource Management. She is also the Director of the Lufthansa General Management Programme, which is a long-term partnership between Lufthansa School of Business and Cranfield School of Management. Her specialist area of interest is cross-cultural management, focusing on the impact of national culture and national context on managerial assumptions and practices.

**Elaine Farndale** BA MA MCIPD, Research Officer, joined Cranfield School of Management in 1998. She is a graduate of the University of Hull (French and Modern Dutch Studies) and Kingston University (Personnel Management). She worked previously in personnel management with the University of London for several years (King's College London and Royal Holloway). Her specialist areas of interest and research include European comparative HRM, HRM and information technology and personnel management in universities. She is currently studying for her PhD and is a Director for leadership and management development programmes for international groups run at Cranfield.

**Ariane Hegewisch** BSc (Econ) MPhil, Lecturer in European Human Resource Management, joined Cranfield in 1989. Her previous experience was in economic and labour market policies in local government. At Cranfield she was a founding researcher of the Cranet (formerly Price Waterhouse Cranfield) Survey on International Strategic HRM. She has co-written a number of books on European HRM and has also published on aspects of European HRM such as remuneration policies, flexible working practices, equal opportunities and employee relations. Her current interests centre on HRM in Europe's public services.

**Gene Johnson** BA MSc PhD, Visiting Fellow, has been involved with Cranet since 1996, when he became the director of the New Zealand portion of the survey. He is an industrial-organizational psychologist, having received his PhD from Tulane University in New Orleans. Formerly a lecturer in the University of Auckland's Management and Employment Relations Department, he taught HRM and organizational psychology. He is currently a management consultant in London, with particular interests in the professionalization of HRM and HR devolution.

**Jos van Ommeren** MSc PhD is Senior Researcher in European HRM at the Centre for European HRM in the Cranfield School of Management. He obtained his MSc in Econometrics at the London School of Economics. Before receiving his PhD in Economics, he worked for a merchant bank in Amsterdam, specializing in corporate finance. His publications are in the field of HRM, labour economics and transport information systems. He has also worked as an academic at the Dutch Central Bank, University College London and the European University Institute in Florence, and has given advice on statistical issues to management consultants.

# Contents

# List of tables

# Cranfield School of Management Research Reports Series

*The Cranfield School of Management Research Reports* series is a major new initiative from Cranfield School of Management and Financial Times Prentice Hall.

The series combines the best in primary research from one of the world's foremost management schools with the traditional publishing and marketing skills of Financial Times Prentice Hall. The reports are designed to allow senior managers to apply the lessons from this research to their own organisations in order to promote best practice across a range of industries.

For further information on other titles in the series, please contact Financial Times Prentice Hall on + 44 (0) 1704 508080 or visit www.briefingzone.com.

## Editorial Board

Professor Alan Harrison, Professor of Operations and Logistics, Exel Research Fellow, Cranfield School of Management

Professor Malcolm McDonald, Professor of Marketing Strategy and Deputy Director, Cranfield School of Management

Gill Marshall, Director, Corporate Communications, Cranfield School of Management

Professor Sudi Sudarsanam, Professor of Finance and Corporate Control, Cranfield School of Management

Professor David Tranfield, Professor of Management, Director of Research and Deputy Director, Cranfield School of Management

Professor Shaun Tyson (Chairman), Professor of Human Resource Management and Head of the Strategic Human Resources Group, Cranfield School of Management

Professor Susan Vinnicombe, Professor of Organisational Behaviour and Diversity Management and Director of Graduate Research, Cranfield School of Management

# 1

# Introduction

T his report is about change in the practice of human resources management (HRM) in the last decade. Back in 1989, when researchers at the Cranfield School of Management and four other European universities, at that time in partnership with Price Waterhouse, founded what was to become the Cranet project, a great deal of change was expected in the field of human resources. Economies were restructuring in response to the decline in manufacturing and the emergence of knowledge-intensive industries. Governments were deregulating, opening up new markets and paving the way for new competitors, both domestic and foreign. New communication technology, including the internet, was further expanding globalization. At the same time, labour markets were changing, with radical shifts in the balance of labour supply and demand, demographic changes in the composition of the labour force, and a marked decline in the influence of trade unions. Last, though not least, the preparations for the single European market were in full swing, and put the comparative advantages – or disadvantages – of the British way of employing people under the microscope. Corporate survival in such a hectic environment required skilful strategies that differentiated one's products or services from the countless others competing for the same business. Inherent to any strategy was a vital resource – the *human* resource.

The realization that people are the key to success – or failure – was not a new one. Decades before, management theory had shown that it was not always money that motivated people to perform (the economic view), nor just social relationships (the human relations' perspective). The human resources movement starting in the 1950s understood that motivation is complex and that people are also motivated to develop themselves and to be challenged by their work. However, it was not until the 1980s that such writings as *In Search of Excellence* by Peters and Waterman (1982) placed emphasis on how motivated, talented employees could be used to competitive advantage; a human resource not easily imitated by competitors, a value-added resource. As service and knowledge-intensive industries and work expanded in importance, so too did the awareness of the value of the employees' contribution. Thus, perhaps for the first time, employees were seen as the key resource within organizations. With the new focus, significant changes were expected. Indeed, the personnel role was expected to transform itself into a valued strategic function.

This expected transformation was the impetus for the Cranet Survey on International Strategic HRM. The survey measures HR policies and practice within organizations around the UK and Europe, and now, indeed, much further afield. The survey's longitudinal design – it is now in its fifth round – provides a series of snapshots of developments in the field of HRM. Its European comparative component – which has grown from the original five to over 30 countries globally – allows us to check whether Europeanization and indeed globalization are eroding the importance of borders in employment practices or are, if not reinforcing, maintaining distinct national patterns of employment. For practitioners, the survey provides benchmarks with which they can compare their own to other organizations' practices. For practitioners, policy makers and academics, the survey acts as an audit – an HR health check, if you like, an assessment tool examining strengths and weaknesses, progress and trends.

A primary goal of the Cranet Survey, then, was to assess the transformation from personnel to HR. Rather than just asking employers how strategic their HR practices are, the survey poses several objective proxy measures that provide an overall picture of HR strategy. Chapter 2 in this report deals directly with this theme and assesses whether HRM is merely a symbolic name for the personnel function or a reality. The other chapters then breakdown HRM practices in greater detail, with Chapter 3 examining recruitment and selection activities, and Chapter 4 exploring the issue of flexibility and new working practices. Chapter 5 considers activities in the field of employee development, whilst Chapter 6 looks at employee compensation and benefits and Chapter 7 at employee communication.

## HR BEST PRACTICE: DO WE PRACTISE WHAT IS PREACHED?

The term 'best practice' is often used to denote ideal HR practices or what 'should be', although there is not always complete agreement on what that means. One model maintains that HR best practices are universal and additive, resulting in positive effects regardless of business strategy (Becker & Gerhart, 1996). This approach sees it possible to generalize best practices to all situations, because their underlying guiding principle is that employee performance is valued and rewarded. Thus, best practices empower and develop human resources. Another approach views best practice as the match between HR strategy and business strategy (Tyson & Doherty, 1999), suggesting that HR best practice is what is best for a given business strategy. This contingency approach is known as the resource-based fit model. We have elsewhere suggested a further dimension to this approach (Brewster, 1995): examining HR policies in Europe calls attention to the external environments in which organizations develop their HR policies. Collective bargaining traditions, employment legislation, the system of vocational training and development, the social security and welfare regime – all these influence the parameters for human resources management. The discussion on HRM has rightly emphasized the need for organizations to be more proactive and strategic in the ways they manage people. But it has done this at the cost of recognizing the ways in which organizations are aided and constrained by the environment in which they operate. The results of the Cranet Survey confirm this point again and again: context is the key for understanding HR trends, whether this is sector, size or, most significantly perhaps, national boundaries. Best practice is not any single policy or practice – it is a package and overall approach. Hence it is not easy to copy.

The Cranet Survey has attempted to track a few predicted trends, including HR devolution to line managers, HR outsourcing, decentralization of HR functions, recruitment difficulties, workforce flexibility practices, family-friendly practices, skills shortages, variable pay and direct communication. The extent to which these trends have occurred – or not – are discussed throughout each of the chapters.

*"Context is the key for understanding HR trends, whether this is sector, size or national boundaries"*

When the project began a decade ago, noticeable national differences were observed, often due to country-specific legislation, employee relations and customs. With the advent of the European Union (EU), the up-take of EU directives, and globalization, it was believed that national differences might dwindle and that a distinct European HR practice might emerge, in effect a 'Europeanization' of HR. To assess this, UK figures are compared to an average for the EU, and country variations are discussed as relevant. To add to the usefulness of the data, major sector averages for the 1999 UK data are also provided, allowing more meaningful benchmarks.

## THE CRANET SURVEY

This report draws on original data from the Cranet project covering the period 1990 to 1999. The aims of the Cranet Survey were – and are – ambitious: to provide hard data on HRM policies and practices for practitioners, policy makers and academics; to monitor the effect of the EU on diversity in HRM practices; and to provide concrete pointers about doing business in different countries. The Cranet Survey is the largest and most representative on-going survey of HRM policies and practices in the world. In broad terms the data is representative of organizations of 200 employees or above in the UK and Europe, and has been so for the various rounds of the survey.

The survey is not an opinion survey. In so far as possible the survey asks for factual data (numbers or percentages) or for yes/no answers to factual questions (do you use ... etc.). It is addressed to the most senior HR/personnel specialist within the organization and more than three-quarters of respondents fit this description. The data is collected through a standardized, postal, questionnaire that is sent to personnel directors at organizational level. It covers major areas of HRM policies and practices. The unit of measurement is the organization, defined as the firm, subsidiary, or if the respondent is in a head office, the group in which the respondent works. For the public sector, it refers to the specific local authority, NHS trust, government department or agency.

Concepts and notions of HRM vary across borders; considerable care is taken to ensure that the questionnaire is relevant and comprehensible in each country. Members of the Cranet network input into the design of the questionnaire and identify areas of particular interest for their country. The questionnaire, including all new questions, is piloted separately in each country; and after having been translated into the national language(s) is retranslated by an independent translator to identify any misunderstandings or inconsistencies. Finally, both the academic partners and the expert panels (see below) ensure that the interpretation of the findings reflects the national context.

During each round of the survey, amendments are made to capture new developments. But on the whole, the questionnaire stays unchanged in order to be able to observe developments over time.

## Representativeness by size and sector

The total number of responses for each year is provided in Table 1.1. The sample was considerably larger in 1990 because the questionnaire was re-mailed to personnel managers who had failed to answer; this generated a much higher response rate than in consequent years. The survey was originally designed to include only organizations with at least 200 employees. Such a definition excludes a large share of organizations in many European countries; hence during the last year of the survey the size band was lowered to 100 employees. For the purposes of comparability over time, however, in this report we only include organizations with at least 200 employees.

This report provides comparisons between HR policies and practices in the UK and the EU. The survey includes all EU countries apart from Luxembourg. In broad terms, the responses in each country reflect the underlying population distribution of organizations by size and sector of industry. Response rates vary substantially between countries, from 10 per cent in the larger countries to over 40 per cent in Sweden; providing an average response rate for the EU therefore is not appropriate. The EU average provided in the report is a weighted average of the 14 countries including the UK. Individual country responses were weighted by the underlying number of private companies with at least 250 employees in each country,[1] based on data provided by Eurostat. For a few smaller countries, this number of companies is unknown, and has been estimated based on the size of the workforce. Typically, values of the EU average are hardly affected by the method of weighting.

| | UK 1990 | 1992 | 1995 | 1999 | EU 1999 |
|---|---|---|---|---|---|
| Number of respondents | 2543 | 1248 | 1184 | 912 | 4079 |
| Response rate (%) | 27 | 17 | 21 | 11 | n/a |

**TABLE 1.1**

**Respondents with 200 and more employees**

Over time there has been a clear change in the size distribution of the UK sample: the share of larger organizations has fallen, and has risen for smaller organizations (*see* Table 1.2). In 1990 the median size of sampled organizations was 1050 and 1100 in 1992; by 1995 it had dropped to 725 and increased again to 800 in 1999. These changes are unlikely to be due to problems with the representativeness of the sample,[2] but appear to reflect underlying trends in the UK economy. Questions in the Cranet Survey about past changes in the size of organizations show net reductions in size between 1992 and 1995 and net increases between 1995 and 1999. For this reason we have decided not to weight the data for size.

Importantly, the method of data collection has remained the same during all rounds, so the sampled distribution of organizations by industry sector has not, or has only marginally, changed during the 1990s. Statistical testing,

---

1  Comparative European statistics are only available for 250 employees, not 200 (the Cranet Survey cut-off point).

2  Using the Kruskal Wallis H test.

using chi-square tests, indicates that differences in the sampled distribution of organizations by industry sector are entirely due to sampling error. This justifies our approach not to weight the results by industry sector.

**TABLE 1.2**

**Sample distribution by size (in % of organizations)**

| Number of employees | UK 1990 | 1992 | 1995 | 1999 | EU 1999 |
|---|---|---|---|---|---|
| 200–499 | 23 | 20 | 30 | 36 | 41 |
| 500–999 | 23 | 25 | 25 | 25 | 25 |
| 1000–1999 | 19 | 19 | 16 | 15 | 15 |
| 2000–4999 | 18 | 18 | 16 | 14 | 11 |
| 5000+ | 18 | 18 | 12 | 11 | 8 |

In this report we distinguish between five broad sectors (*see* Table 1.3): manufacturing; other industry (which includes other manufacturing as well as agriculture, energy and water, chemical processing and construction); business services (which includes banking, finance and insurance); other services (which includes transport, wholesale and retail, hotels and catering and other services) and the public sector (which includes public health services, higher education, local and central government).

**TABLE 1.3**

**Sample distribution by sector (in % of organizations)**

| | UK 1990 % (n=) | 1992 % (n=) | 1995 % (n=) | 1999 % (n=) | EU 1999 % (n=) |
|---|---|---|---|---|---|
| Manufacturing | 37 (933) | 34 (425) | 31 (382) | 29 (263) | 41 (1448) |
| Other industry | 10 (253) | 11 (142) | 9 (115) | 6.5 (59) | 14 (475) |
| Business services | 10 (255) | 10 (126) | 11 (140) | 10 ( 92) | 9 (378) |
| Other services | 26 (665) | 17 (210) | 18 (219) | 18 (163) | 15 (596) |
| Public sector | 17 (433) | 26 (329) | 30 (368) | 24 (222) | 15 (606) |
| Missing | 0 (4) | 1 (16) | 2 (22) | 12 (112) | 14 (577) |

## Advisory panel

The representative and comprehensive statistical analysis is enhanced by qualitative comment from an advisory panel of HR directors of leading edge organizations in each country. The panels have between 10 and 20 members. Panel members advise on new topic areas, comment on new questions and meet at least once after each survey round for an in-depth discussion of survey findings in view of experiences in their own organizations.

In sum, this report is a review of the HR function over time, in terms of how it has altered and progressed, both from a UK and a European perspective. Looking back, the project has grown far beyond the dreams of its founders and has become an essential source of data on comparative HRM, for researchers and practitioners alike. As a snapshot of the HR profession, the survey and this report describe HR practice as it now exists. As such, they should be evidence of success in HR strategy and best practice where these are in place, and an incentive to change where needed.

*"The survey should be evidence of success in HR strategy and best practice and an incentive to change where needed"*

## REFERENCES

Becker, B. & Gerhart, B. (1996) 'The impact of human resource management on organizational performance: progress and prospects', *Academy of Management Journal*, 39 (4), pp. 779–801.

Brewster, C. (1995) 'HRM: The European dimension' in J. Storey (ed.) *Human Resource Management: A critical text*. London: Routledge, pp. 309–31.

Peters, T. & Waterman, R. (1982) *In Search of Excellence*. New York: Harper & Row.

Tyson, S. & Doherty, N. (1999) *Human Resource Excellence Report*. London: Financial Times Management.

# 2

# The changing roles of HR

## EXECUTIVE SUMMARY

Chapter 2 examines how the HR function may have changed over the past decade, looking at HR strategy, devolution, outsourcing, and decentralization v. centralization.

The main findings are:

- HR functions are taken seriously by UK organizations. Nearly all employers with 200+ employees have a formal HR function, and three-quarters of the most senior HR staff members are HR-experienced when put into that role.

- (HR integration – the extent to which HR issues are considered as part of business strategy development – is only moderate and has not improved over the decade.) Only roughly half of UK organizations place HR on the board of directors and involve HR from the outset in corporate strategy development.

- There has been a significant increase in the number of organizations with formal HR strategies, yet still only six out of ten workplaces have them.

- Only four out of ten employers conduct evaluations of the HR function to see how well it is doing.

- Public-sector employers are consistently more advanced on the above indicators than other employers, suggesting that they are more advanced in HR formalization and strategy.

- The UK compares favourably on HR strategy measures with the EU average, although there are individual country variations.

- Contrary to expectations, there is no clear HR devolution trend. While line managers increasingly take on HR roles, the partnership between HR and line managers has remained the same over time: a consultative one, with HR providing the direction.

- HR staff-to-employee ratios have declined, not increased, being further evidence against HR devolution. The UK ratio for 1999 is one HR staff for every 83 employees, down from 113 in 1990.

- HR outsourcing is quite common in UK workplaces, and most common for training and development. Public-sector employers are least likely to take advantage of HR outsourcing.

- There is no across-the-board move to HR decentralization or centralization. Rather, it appears to depend upon the HR policy areas.

Financially sensitive matters are apt to be centralized. Also, manufacturing firms are the most likely to have decentralized functions.

## INTRODUCTION

The popular literature tells us that HR roles are changing in line with organizations' constant battle to keep up with the competition or to lead the way. The economic environment of the last two decades can be described as extremely competitive, due to developments in technology and electronic communications; the subsequent opening of larger markets to new entrants, including international ones; and additional worldwide deregulation of industries and markets. As organizations compete with others to sell their wares, focus has been placed on both cost efficiency and the valuing of human resources. The former aims to cut out excess costs and emphasizes value-added services and products. The latter realizes that value-added resources are often *human*; that is, it is employee contributions that can make or break an organization. This has become particularly evident in service and knowledge-intensive industries, where organizational possession of inimitable employee knowledge and skills is a competitive advantage. Whether attention is focused on cost efficiency or valuing human resources, or indeed on both, an HR strategy is needed; thus requiring HR functions to become more strategic.

Historically, it is assumed that 'people' functions in organizations – in the form of the personnel department – have not been strategic but primarily administrative. They were seen as reactive to business strategy, rather than proactive; short-term focused; and operational (i.e. implementing and 'fire-fighting'). In effect, the traditional personnel function was criticized as not taking the human resource seriously enough, not contributing to profits, and not aligned with corporate objectives. In the new economic environment, the personnel function is pressured to evolve into a strategic role, the 'HR' function, with the new name symbolizing its strategic nature. In this idealized mode, the HR function proactively contributes to corporate strategy, is long-term focused, and casts off most of its operational and implementation roles in favour of strategic and advisory ones. In essence, it is integrated with business strategy. Obviously, a match between business strategy and HR strategy is best practice.

Strategic redirection of the HR function may result in other trends that impact on how the HR function operates. One of these trends is the supposed increased responsibility of line managers for HR roles, known as devolution. This is in line with managers taking more responsibility for the human resources with which they work so closely. In turn, HR staff are meant to advise managers on how they best carry out these roles. Another trend is outsourcing, or devolvement of some HR responsibilities to external contractors. Any outsourced roles would be deemed as non-value-added and/or more efficiently performed outside the organization. A third trend is the decentralization of HR functions. Current best-practice thinking is that HR departments should function autonomously within the operational units of a larger organization. However, there are the risks of resource inefficiency (e.g. the same functions doing the same work in different units) and of straying from strategy. It might be that best practice is the centralization of some functions and the decentralization of others.)

If the HR function is changing and becoming more strategic, the Cranet Surveys over the past decade (from 1990 to 1999) should reflect any progress made. In addition, these data can act as benchmarks for HR directors to guide future strategy and practice. This chapter first examines to what extent HR functions have become strategic arms of the organization. This is done through examining several proxies for strategy, including formal signs of strategy and influence. Next, the other trends (devolution of HR roles to line managers, outsourcing, and decentralization v. centralization) are reviewed to see how they, in turn, might be changing HR roles.

## FROM PERSONNEL TO HRM: HOW STRATEGIC IS THE HR FUNCTION?

How do we measure progress toward the idealized HR function? Asking survey respondents to rate the extent to which their HR functions are strategic would be a failure, as social desirability would win out over objectivity. Instead, the Cranet Survey presents various 'proxy' measures that represent different strategic indicators. While they may not be able to measure the exact extent of HR strategy, they at least indicate HR strategy-formalization attempts. These strategic indicators are:

- the presence of a formal HR department and/or HR manager and background of the most senior HR person – reflecting the initial seriousness with which organizations take their human resources;

- a place on the board of directors for the HR function and involvement in developing corporate strategy – indicating integration, or the degree to which HR issues are considered as part of business strategy development;

- the development of a written HR strategy and of specific HR policies – attesting to actual HR strategy development;

- whether the HR function is formally evaluated – signifying whether the function is valued enough to be tracked.

It should be noted that the term 'HR' used throughout this report refers to both formal HR departments and less formal HR functions and roles, whether organizations label them as 'personnel' or 'HR'.

*"Without influence, it is difficult to contribute to corporate strategy or implement HR strategy"*

### How seriously is the HR function taken?

Two very basic indicators of how seriously the HR function is taken are the presence of an HR department and/or HR manager and whether the most senior HR manager comes from an HR background. The former attests to an organization's initial attempts to manage HR formally, while the latter assumes that for HR issues to be skilfully managed, the person leading the function should have experience in the HR field. While positive signs of these may not necessarily indicate HR strategy, their absence may reflect that HR is not taken seriously and thus cannot have influence. Without influence, it is difficult to contribute to corporate strategy or implement HR strategy.

Both measures produce quite positive results. The Cranet Surveys have consistently shown throughout the 1990s that nearly all UK organizations with 200+ employees have a formal HR function or HR manager – 99 per cent in 1999. The 1999 EU average is pretty much the same. As for the most senior HR person's background, throughout much of the 1990s about three-quarters of UK organizations have ensured that the person filling this role comes with HR experience. This is fortunate evidence that the practice of rotating non-HR people through the function, because 'anyone can be a good people manager, and thus a good HR manager' (Downie & Coates, 1995), is not as common as thought. However, there are some differences by UK sectors. In particular, one-third of public-sector employers is apt to place non-HR people in top HR roles, compared to only 19 per cent in the financial and business sector. Still, the UK fares well compared to the EU averages, where only 62 per cent of organizations place HR-trained people in the most senior roles. Indeed, in countries like Finland and Austria, less than half of organizations do so.

## HR integration

As defined above, HR integration is the degree to which HR issues are considered as part of business strategy development (Brewster & Holt Larsen, 1992). A truly integrated HR function would be an equal business partner with the other corporate functions, and work in unison with corporate strategy. As mentioned earlier, HR representatives must be core members of the team of strategic decision makers. If they are included as an afterthought or as mere implementers, their traditional reactive role remains unchanged. Thus, two proxies indicate integration:

- HR representation on the main policy-making body (e.g. board of directors)
- the extent to which HR representatives are involved in developing corporate strategy.

### Board representation

A place on the board or equivalent is the forum for inclusion in strategic decision making. It can be argued that if HR is not on the board, HR issues might not be considered appropriately, just as a discussion on financial issues would be lacking without the chief financial officer. That is, representation by other senior officials, such as the CEO, would not permit the necessary insight into and expertise on HR issues. Furthermore, membership of the board signals HR's status and provides opportunities for influence.

Of course, there is the alternative argument that board representation does not equal influence and strategy involvement, even if it is desirable (Kochan & Dyer, 1995; Storey, 1995). As put by Ward Griffiths (2000), Assistant Director of the CIPD, 'Board membership itself does not equate to influence'. Furthermore, the executive director of a large UK-owned fashion retailer believes that 'the board is a formal operation. Most of the work is done outside. If we are talking about how decisions get made, the HR person might be more influential in an informal role.' Indeed, some would assert that the role played by HR in influencing boardroom decisions is more the direct result of the HR director's character and individual standing rather than board presence, but certainly this could apply to any manager. Perhaps a test of this argument is whether other functions, such as finance or marketing, could operate effectively without a presence on the board.

Currently, just under half (49 per cent) of UK organizations save a place for HR on their boards or equivalent decision-making bodies; this has declined gradually at each survey from a high of 63 per cent in 1990. When the HR function does not have a seat on the board, it is the chief executive who most likely represents HR issues. Public-sector employers are most likely (54 per cent) to include HR, whereas business service organizations are least likely (41 per cent). While the proportion of UK organizations with HR inclusion may seem close to the EU average of 55 per cent, it is actually much lower than the approximately eight in ten organizations in France, Sweden, Belgium and Spain. However, there are countries that are even less likely to include HR, such as Portugal, Greece, Italy, the Netherlands and Austria, where only about 30 to 40 per cent of workplaces include HR on the board.

The Cranet data are supported by research by Sisson (1995), who reported that only half of UK organizations had any kind of representation on senior management committees and the like. However, the data are lower than other estimates, which report a figure closer to 70 per cent. For example, Tyson and Doherty (1999) report 68 per cent of organizations (from 500 to 500 000 employees), from a sample of 50, with HR on the board. Still, this is a self-selected sample of best-practice employers, as they were entrants for an HR excellence award. The Cranet data are a much larger sample, and board inclusion could very well be a matter of organizational size. As the number of employees increases, so does board inclusion. So, for workplaces with 201–500 employees, 41 per cent seat include HR on the board, compared to 53 per cent for 501–5000, and 55 per cent for 5000+. The 1998 Workplace Employee Relations Survey, which includes a higher proportion of smaller organizations, shows a figure somewhere between the Tyson and the Cranet data (Culley et al, 1999).

### Corporate strategy involvement

Involvement in developing corporate strategy is a corollary to board status, although can certainly occur without being on the board. Similar to board inclusion, HR's involvement in developing corporate strategy is moderate. The ultimate integration – involvement from the outset as an equal contributor – has hovered around the 50-per-cent mark throughout the past decade and currently stands at 54 per cent. A further third of UK organizations take a lesser, consultative role, and fewer than one in ten organizations (8 per cent) act as mere implementers of corporate strategy. Only 6 per cent report having no involvement whatsoever. There is a marked difference in HR involvement between the different market sectors. The HR director, or equivalent, is almost twice as likely to be involved from the outset in corporate strategy development in the public sector (66 per cent) than in business service workplaces (35 per cent) (*see* Table 2.1).

| | UK 1999 Manufac-turing | Other industry | Business services | Other services | Public sector | UK average | EU 1999 EU average |
|---|---|---|---|---|---|---|---|
| From the outset | 48 | 53 | 35 | 61 | 66 | 54 | 58 |
| Consultative | 33 | 28 | 49 | 24 | 29 | 33 | 24 |
| Implementer | 13 | 8 | 10 | 7 | 3 | 8 | 10 |
| Not consulted | 7 | 13 | 6 | 8 | 2 | 6 | 8 |

**TABLE 2.1**

**Involvement of HR in the development of corporate strategy, by sector (in % of organizations)**

The EU average for HR involvement is 58 per cent. In contrast to the wide disparity between countries in HR inclusion on the board of directors, there is little national variance for involvement in corporate strategy development. The UK again finds itself slightly under the EU average, but there are no radical leaders or laggards. Surprisingly, Italian workplaces are the most likely for HR involvement at the outset (68 per cent), considering they are very unlikely to have board HR representation. As may be expected, countries like Greece and Portugal are the least likely for HR involvement in developing corporate strategy (about 50 per cent).

### Board presence as influence

At first glance, it might seem that board presence and strategy involvement, at best moderate, do not tell us much about HR's influence within organizations. However, a deeper look reveals that a seat on the board of directors might be the pivotal point from which HR does exert influence. In organizations where the HR function holds a place on the board or equivalent, over seven out of ten (74 per cent) organizations report involvement in corporate strategic decision making from the outset. This is more than twice the number of organizations where HR does not sit on the board (33 per cent). This pattern is seen in most UK sectors (e.g. other services, 87 per cent; public sector, 81 per cent), although less so in the business services, where still only 44 per cent are involved from the outset.

## HR strategy and policy development

The third set of proxies relate to HR strategy itself; that is, is HR strategy developed in line with corporate strategy, and are specific HR policies evolved from the strategy? To assess how much progress organizations have made over the 1990s in forming HR strategy, it is first necessary to know how well organizations are doing in formalizing corporate strategies, from which HR strategies are derived. The Cranet Survey asks about mission statements, which are meant to reflect an organization's vision, and corporate strategy. Formal, written strategy statements are considered imperative, if they are to be taken seriously. UK organizations have made great progress here throughout the 1990s, with steady increases to the current plateau, as is evident in Table 2.2. Interestingly, if an organization has one of the formal statements, it is likely to have the others as well. In 1999 almost nine out of ten (88 per cent) UK organizations with a written mission statement also had a written corporate strategy. Sector percentages are displayed in Table 2.3.

**TABLE 2.2**

**Organizations with formal written statements (in %)**

|  | UK 1990 | 1992 | 1995 | 1999 | EU 1999 |
|---|---|---|---|---|---|
| Mission statement | 53 | 68 | 81 | 83 | 71 |
| Corporate strategy | 67 | 73 | 79 | 83 | 67 |
| HR strategy | 46 | 53 | 60 | 61 | 45 |

**TABLE 2.3**

**Organizations with formal written statements by sector (in %)**

|  | UK 1999 Manufacturing | Other industry | Business services | Other services | Public sector |
|---|---|---|---|---|---|
| Mission statement | 80 | 77 | 75 | 84 | 93 |
| Corporate strategy | 75 | 86 | 88 | 80 | 91 |
| HR strategy | 51 | 58 | 65 | 59 | 71 |

### HR strategy

Using the proportion of organizations that have mission statements and business strategies in place as a benchmark comparison, it is evident that organizations have not embraced formal HR strategies to the same extent (*see* Table 2.2). While there has been significant improvement over the past ten years, development of HR strategy is still only at a moderate level, at which it appears to have plateaued. Sector differences (*see* Table 2.3) are also obvious, with the public sector again leading the pack. As expected, in most workplaces (nearly 70 per cent), having an HR strategy is preceded by having a written mission statement and/or corporate strategy, in that the former is ideally, strategically derived from the latter.

Current UK levels of formal strategy development compare favourably to the European averages (see Table 2.2). Indeed, the average proportion of European organizations with formal HR strategies is near that exhibited in the UK in 1990 (45 per cent). Of course, there are country differences. The leaders in developing formal HR strategies include Sweden, the Netherlands, Finland, Denmark and the UK (from 60 to 70 per cent). Well below average are Germany and Austria, with only three of every ten workplaces developing written HR strategies.

### HR policies

A further formalization of HR strategy is the development of specific policy, which in turn acts as the formal guidelines for practice. The Cranet Survey has asked about policy development for specific HR sub-functions or areas since 1995. Between then and now, activity has been generally static. Table 2.4 provides the UK overall and sector averages for 1999. The areas most commonly addressed by policy are equal opportunity (EO)/diversity (88 per cent) and training and development (83 per cent). The former finding is quite a surprise, but probably due to government legislation relating to gender, race and disability. At least this will be encouraging to those bodies working to further the management of diversity in UK workplaces, who have generally argued that formalization is the first step towards progress.

| | UK 1999 | | | | | | EU 1999 |
| | Manufac-turing | Other industry | Business services | Other services | Public sector | UK average | EU average |
| --- | --- | --- | --- | --- | --- | --- | --- |
| Pay and benefits | 52 | 73 | 65 | 64 | 69 | 62 | 65 |
| Recruitment and selection | 65 | 72 | 69 | 75 | 95 | 77 | 51 |
| Training and development | 77 | 83 | 86 | 81 | 92 | 83 | 68 |
| Communication | 50 | 55 | 40 | 48 | 48 | 49 | 38 |
| Equal opportunity/ diversity | 80 | 91 | 89 | 89 | 98 | 88 | 37 |
| Flexibility | 32 | 29 | 32 | 28 | 61 | 38 | 47 |
| Management development | 44 | 57 | 43 | 48 | 53 | 49 | 38 |

**TABLE 2.4**

**Written policy development by sector (in % of organizations)**

As for training policies, most focus on who receives training and to what extent (e.g. number of days). The least likely issue to be formalized with policy is labour-market flexibility – that is, varying employee contracts, work schedules, and work locations to meet work and project demands. This seems at odds with the supposed popularity of flexible schemes used in workplaces, suggesting that many flexible options are informally practised. Indeed, a further 23 per cent of employers report having 'unwritten' policies on flexibility.

Sector differences abound here. Public-sector organizations are more likely to develop policies than the average UK workplace on all but communication issues. Particularly striking is their leadership on developing flexibility policies, perhaps reflecting their coping strategy for recruitment and retention difficulties. On the other side of the spectrum are manufacturing firms, who are the least likely in most areas to develop policies.

*"A formal evaluation signifies that HR activities are valued enough to have their outcomes tracked"*

In comparison to the European averages, UK organizations are more likely to develop policies for most of the areas in Table 2.4. The most striking difference is that for EO/diversity, mostly due to the lack of EO legislation in many other countries. In only one area, pay and benefits, does the European average equal that of the UK, and in only one, flexibility, does it lead. Obviously, country differences do exist around the average. For example, the Netherlands has the highest proportion of organizations with written HR policies for pay and recruitment, the UK for training, Finland for communication, and Sweden for equal opportunities.

One reason for the higher use of formal policy in the UK may be the extent to which legal instruments govern corporate activity in other countries, such as in Germany, reducing the need or opportunity for company-specific policies. This may change as increasing harmonization of statutory requirements takes place within the EU. Other factors affecting the extent of policy writing may include the prevailing authority culture, average company sizes, or the share of public-sector organizations in the national sample.

## Evaluating the HR function

The last strategy proxy is the extent to which HR functions are formally evaluated, which is useful in two ways. First, a formal evaluation signifies that HR activities are valued enough to have their outcomes tracked. Second, evaluation provides concrete evidence of the function's contribution to organizational success. In 1999 less than half (44 per cent) of all UK organizations conducted a formal evaluation of their HR functions. This number has remained relatively stable over the decade. The sectors do not vary much from this average, although manufacturing operations are the least likely to invest in the time and resources to evaluate the function (35 per cent), compared to half of all other-industry and public-sector organizations. The European average (40 per cent) is not much less than the UK average. The countries most likely to have workplaces evaluating their HR departments/functions are unexpected: Italy (71 per cent) and Greece (64 per cent), considering their placement on the measures already discussed. Organizations least likely to evaluate the function tend to be found in Sweden, Austria, Finland, Denmark and Germany (about 20 to 30 per cent).

## Summary

So, how do UK organizations fare when it comes to HR strategy? Has there been much progress over the past decade? While it is quite obvious that the HR function is taken seriously by organizations, no real progress has been made over time. HR integration continues to occur in only half of workplaces, with no signs of growth. The development of HR strategy has increased significantly, but has also appeared to plateau. Finally, less than half of workplaces take the time to evaluate their HR functions. Compared to the EU average, UK organizations generally perform favourably, but as a country the UK is no obvious strategy leader. In fact there are no clear front-runners among the EU nations. Most countries do not display uniform signs of strategy across the different measures. In terms of UK sector differences, public-sector employers consistently show more signs of strategic HR than others, and manufacturers tend to show the least signs of HR formalization.

The foregoing indicators show no great change in the extent of strategic involvement or formalization of HR strategy throughout the 1990s. Other researchers and studies have come to the same conclusion, suggesting that for many organizations 'HR' continues to be merely a symbolic label and not a real indicator of strategic activity (Brewster, 1995; Brewster & Hegewisch, 1994; Storey, 1995; Towers-Perrin, 1992). Why might this be? One proposal is that formal HR strategy may appear inflexible, so organizations and the people that run them are reluctant to put their plans on paper. Another is that strategy development takes time and resources, and the pay-offs are not immediately certain (Pfeffer, 1996). Indeed, HR has historically been viewed as a cost to be minimized and not as a source of value creation (Becker & Gerhart, 1996). However, both proposals are invalid, considering that other organizational resources are not so informally managed. Essentially, it may come down to the inability of HR staff to sell their ideas, due to lack of influence (Pfeffer, 1996).

## OGANIZATIONAL TRENDS AFFECTING THE HR FUNCTION AND ROLES

Thus, HR roles are changing (or, at least meant to be) as the function attempts to become more strategic. What other factors may have influenced how HR roles are changing? During the 1990s the academic and popular literatures were concerned with three other trends or issues:

- HR roles of line managers and devolution
- outsourcing
- centralization v. decentralization.

From a strategic perspective, activity in these areas might indicate an organization thoughtfully managing its human resources. On the other hand, they might be seen as indicators of improved cost effectiveness, implying that human resources are not valued, so they are expendable.

### Assignment/devolution

As HR functions attempt to become more strategic, the corollary is that they will also become more policy-oriented and advisory, sharing responsibility with line managers for creating HR policy. Also forcing these changes is the notion that HR decisions should be pushed closer to line managers, because such decisions are too critical to be left to the HR function alone (Storey, 1995). Two relevant terms here are assignment and devolution. The allocation of primary responsibility for HR policy is known as assignment. The transferral of duties from the HR function to line managers is known as devolution. Over time, as devolution occurs, we would expect increasing assignment of HR roles to line managers.

#### Assignment

One way in which the Cranet data explore whether devolution is occurring is to chart changes in line managers' policy assignment over time. Thus, changing assignment infers devolution. The most common pattern, unchanged over time, is a sharing of responsibilities between HR and line managers, albeit that in most areas (pay and benefits, training and development, industrial relations, and health and safety) HR takes the dominant role in the partnership, relying upon line management in consultation. This is consistent with other research findings (IPD, 1995; Sisson, 1995). There is only one policy area where responsibility appears to be changing over time – recruitment and selection – and line managers' involvement is gradually decreasing (*see* Table 2.5). There is also only one policy area where line management directs the relationship – workforce adjustment (e.g. expansion, downsizing). This might infer that when it comes to financially critical decisions, HR takes the back seat. In sum, in most organizations there are no areas where line managers or HR staff solely dominate.

| | UK 1992 | 1995 | 1999 | EU 1999 |
|---|---|---|---|---|
| Line management | 6 | 4 | 4 | 7 |
| Line management in consultation with HR | 40 | 37 | 33 | 40 |
| HR in consultation with line management | 44 | 46 | 48 | 43 |
| HR department | 11 | 12 | 15 | 11 |

**TABLE 2.5**
**Primary responsibility for major policy decisions on recruitment and selection (in % of organizations)**

Although the same pattern is obvious across the sectors, there are two noticeable trends. Compared to the other sectors, line managers' policy responsibilities are enhanced in the non-manufacturing industries (e.g. building and transportation), usually in consultation with HR. In contrast, service industries other than financial and business tend to rely more upon HR staff.

Compared to the UK, the EU averages for each policy area indicate a greater role for line managers (*see* Table 2.6), particularly regarding pay and benefits, recruitment and selection, and training. However, the real picture shows a divide between two camps. On one side, where the UK presides, are those countries that rely more on HR in consultation with line management (e.g. Ireland, France and Portugal). On the other side are those countries relying more on line management in consultation with HR (e.g. Sweden, Denmark, Netherlands, Finland and Austria). It is perhaps ironic that the UK sits where it does, given that the role of line managers in HRM has probably been more discussed in the UK than anywhere else in Europe.

**TABLE 2.6**

**Primary responsibility for major policy decisions (in % of organizations) (1999)**

| | Pay and benefits | | Recruitment and selection | | Training and development | | Industrial relations | | Workforce adjustment | |
|---|---|---|---|---|---|---|---|---|---|---|
| | UK | EU | UK | EU | UK | EU | UK | EU | UK | EU |
| Line management | 5 | 8 | 4 | 7 | 4 | 7 | 3 | 8 | 12 | 12 |
| Line management in consultation with HR | 25 | 36 | 33 | 40 | 30 | 38 | 22 | 20 | 50 | 43 |
| HR in consultation with line management | 52 | 41 | 48 | 43 | 54 | 44 | 50 | 36 | 31 | 34 |
| HR department | 18 | 16 | 15 | 11 | 13 | 11 | 25 | 36 | 7 | 11 |

As found with earlier results, inclusion of HR on the board appears to enhance the HR function's influence. Where an HR representative is on the board, the HR function is more likely to maintain primary control of HR policy decisions (*see* Table 2.7). Where HR is not on the board, line management has more control over these decisions. For example, when HR is on the board, 23 per cent of line managers direct pay and benefits policy (including with HR consultation). Without HR on the board, this rises to 38 per cent. Sector results display this even more emphatically. For example, in 23 per cent of manufacturing organizations, line managers take the lead on pay and benefits policy making when HR is on the board, versus 40 per cent when not.

**TABLE 2.7**

**Primary responsibility for major policy decisions as a function of HR presence on the board (in % of organizations) (UK 1999)**

| | Pay and benefits | | Recruitment and selection | | Training and development | | Industrial relations | | Workforce adjustment | |
|---|---|---|---|---|---|---|---|---|---|---|
| | On board | Not on | On board | Not on | On board | Not on | On board | Not on | On board | Not on |
| Line management | 2 | 8 | 3 | 5 | 3 | 4 | 2 | 4 | 10 | 13 |
| Line management in consultation with HR | 21 | 30 | 30 | 34 | 27 | 32 | 17 | 26 | 45 | 55 |
| HR in consultation with line management | 58 | 46 | 53 | 44 | 59 | 50 | 55 | 46 | 38 | 25 |
| HR department | 19 | 17 | 13 | 17 | 12 | 14 | 26 | 25 | 7 | 7 |

## Devolution

An alternative check on whether devolution is a reality is the extent to which respondents report increases or decreases in line responsibilities over the past few years, in terms of changing roles. Although significant increases have been reported throughout the decade, the majority report no change in responsibility, with the exception of training and development. At each survey in 1992 and 1995, roughly half of respondents have increased line managers' training and development duties; this proportion dropped slightly to 41 per cent in 1999. Increases in other areas were reported by no more than about a quarter: pay and benefits (23 per cent), recruitment and selection (29 per cent), industrial relations (19 per cent), and workforce adjustment (25 per cent). It should be noted that contrary to our earlier assignment finding, few workplaces report a decline in line management involvement in recruitment and selection (only 6 per cent in 1999).

### HR ratio

A third possible measure of devolution is the HR staff-to-employee ratio, or the number of employees supported per HR staff member. One assumption of devolution is that as line managers take on HR roles, fewer HR staff are needed. One problem with this assumption is that it does not take into account HR staff's expanded roles as strategists and policy advisors. Also, a reduced HR staff might simply result from a downsizing exercise divorced from devolution or any strategic approach. In any case, the HR staff-to-employee ratio is a widely used benchmark. The evidence shows that the ratio of HR staff relative to the total number of employees has progressively declined over the last decade (*see* Table 2.8). The current median is one HR staff member for every 83 employees, similar to that for the EU.

*"HR staff sizes appear to have increased instead of decreased, contrary to what would be expected with devolution"*

|  | UK 1990 | 1992 | 1995 | 1999 | EU 1999 |
|---|---|---|---|---|---|
|  | 113 | 90 | 90 | 83 | 80 |
| Median organizational size | 1050 | 1100 | 725 | 800 | 600 |

**TABLE 2.8**
HR staff-to-employee ratio

Thus HR staff sizes appear to have increased instead of decreased, contrary to what would be expected with devolution. However, the HR staff-to-employee ratio is often a function of organizational size or number of employees. Note in Table 2.8 that the median organizational size has decreased considerably since 1992. Table 2.9 further emphasizes the impact of organizational size, as the ratio expands with larger organizations. Could it be that what appears to be devolution is just smaller organizations unable to afford HR staff? Still, the medians for 1992 and 1995 (from

Table 2.8) are the same, regardless of organizational size. Also, the countries with the largest ratios have considerably different median organizational sizes: Sweden (1:104, median 776 employees), Denmark (1:107, median 479 employees). Indeed, the EU country with the lowest ratio (1:60), the Netherlands, has a median in between those two (627 employees). Thus, organizational size does not entirely explain the ratio.

**TABLE 2.9**

**Median HR staff-to-employee ratio by organizational size (UK 1999)**

| Organizational size (number of employees) | | | | |
| --- | --- | --- | --- | --- |
| 200–499 | 500–999 | 1000–1999 | 2000–4999 | 5000+ |
| 68 | 81 | 92 | 114 | 159 |

Sector could be another factor, as there are some differences (*see* Table 2.10). Sector ratios are probably influenced by the predominance of service and knowledge-intensive jobs. That is, these jobs may require more HR guidance, as they are more complex and employees are more skilled than in traditional production jobs. This is evident in the contrast between the ratios for financial and business services and manufacturing and other industries (58 v. 90–100 employees per HR staff member). Another factor might be the degree of change experienced by organizations; as organizations restructure and downsize, more HR staff are needed to introduce and maintain new systems.

**TABLE 2.10**

**Median HR staff-to-employee ratio by sector**

| | UK 1999 Manufacturing | Other industry | Business services | Other services | Public sector |
| --- | --- | --- | --- | --- | --- |
| | 90 | 100 | 58 | 86 | 78 |
| Median organizational size | 550 | 630 | 762 | 758 | 743 |

In sum, there are no clear signs that HR devolution is occurring. Most HR responsibilities are shared by the HR function and line management. In the majority of UK workplaces the balance of this partnership is unchanged, even considering a significant number of line managers taking on HR roles. Furthermore, HR staff-to-employee ratios are declining and not increasing as would be expected. Despite this conclusion, it must be said that many HR practitioners are adamant that HR devolution is occurring. Thus, it remains for practitioners to look within to see if devolution is a reality and for researchers to come up with better devolution measures.

## Outsourcing HR activities

Outsourcing derives from the belief that organizations can be run more cost-effectively by contracting external sources to manage non-value-added functions, while the organization focuses on the value-added ones. Ideally, outsourcing is part of a long-term strategic plan. In reality, it may merely be part of a cost-cutting exercise focused on the short term. The idea of outsourcing the entire HR function is not a likelihood in most organizations, as there is general agreement that HR is too strategic to leave to outsiders (Davidson, 1998). However, outsourcing of various HR functions is quite common in UK organizations. In 1999 only one in ten (11 per cent) HR departments did not make some use of external provision (*see* Table 2.11).

| | UK 1999 Manufac- turing | Other industry | Business services | Other services | Public sector | UK average | EU 1999 EU average |
|---|---|---|---|---|---|---|---|
| Pay and benefits | 29 | 36 | 43 | 29 | 29 | 32 | 28 |
| Recruitment and selection | 65 | 71 | 61 | 45 | 20 | 49 | 56 |
| Training and development | 87 | 89 | 90 | 78 | 68 | 81 | 70 |
| Workforce expansion and reduction | 29 | 36 | 49 | 23 | 13 | 26 | 22 |
| No external providers used | 6 | 11 | 5 | 13 | 18 | 11 | 13 |

**TABLE 2.11**

**Use of external providers of HR services by sector (in % of organizations)**

The area most commonly outsourced is training and development, with external training help purchased by 81 per cent of organizations. The extent of outsourcing depends upon both how routine and vital a process might be. For example, most outsourcing in pay and benefits is of the payroll function, as it is quite a standard process. Employers would be less likely to trust the management of salaries, however, to outsiders, considering the significant role of money in reward and motivation. Reliance by companies in the EU upon outsourcing is much the same as in the UK, on average, although there are country variations. In particular, outsourcing is relatively uncommon in Finnish workplaces, with 72 per cent of organizations not practising it. In contrast, Belgian workplaces tend to be the most likely of all the EU countries to outsource pay and benefits, recruitment and selection, and training.

While outsourcing may be quite common in the UK private sector, it is much less so in the public sector. It could be that public-sector employers are more financially constrained. Also, the prevalence of trade unions in the public sector may discourage outsourcing, as it may be seen as a threat to job security of union members. It is also possible that public employers' lower levels of outsourcing reflect a more strategic approach to managing human resources, considering their generally superior performance on the HR strategy indicators discussed earlier. The reverse of this assumption is that many private-sector employers are using outsourcing as a short-term, non-strategic practice. Unfortunately, these assumptions cannot be tested with the Cranet data and remain as mere suggestions. In sum, while outsourcing is quite common in the UK, whether it is used strategically or merely to cut costs is not clearly known.

## Centralization v. decentralization

To decentralize or centralize? – that is the question. As a broad extension of devolution, decentralization brings control of operational and business decisions to individual business units or divisions. This aligns with the notions of autonomy and localization, i.e. policy decision making occurs where policy is implemented. In terms of HR, decentralization usually means that each business unit or organizational division has its own HR function or specialist functions (e.g. training). While decentralization has long been the best-practice ideal, these days it is accused of being costly and detracting from competitive advantage. In particular, it is often seen as a costly duplication of effort and a fragmentation of strategy, organizational communication, and corporate image. As a result, the centralized corporate service centre is advocated (Arkin, 1999). Could it be that either extreme is not necessary and that a compromise approach works best? That is, for some HR issues or functions, localization is quite imperative, hence a decentralized approach is needed; for other areas, a unified, corporate policy or approach is vital, hence decisions are made at headquarters.

There is some evidence that this combined approach occurs in the UK. For most policy matters, there is no dominant approach. Organizations tend to allow policy development at a variety of levels, both centralized and decentralized (see Table 2.12), although there are relatively few decrees sent out from international headquarters. For example, note how roughly one-third of organizations opts for recruitment and selection policy development at the national, subsidiary, and establishment levels. When it comes to direct financial matters, however, organizations are more likely to dictate policy centrally. Note how half of all pay policies are arranged at the national levels. UK organizations are also more apt to dictate management development approaches from both international and national levels, indicating that a unified corporate strategy is desired. This pattern of decision making has been consistent over the 1990s.

| | Pay and benefits | | Recruitment and selection | | Training and development | | Industrial relations | | Workforce adjustment | | Management development | |
|---|---|---|---|---|---|---|---|---|---|---|---|---|
| | UK | EU | UK | EU | UK | EU | UK | EU | UK | EU | UK | EU |
| International HQ | 12 | 15 | 6 | 7 | 7 | 10 | 5 | 7 | 11 | 13 | 15 | 21 |
| National HQ | 50 | 58 | 37 | 45 | 35 | 44 | 37 | 50 | 34 | 46 | 35 | 51 |
| Subsidiary | 19 | 17 | 26 | 29 | 27 | 28 | 24 | 26 | 26 | 26 | 25 | 17 |
| Establishment | 20 | 10 | 31 | 19 | 31 | 18 | 34 | 17 | 28 | 16 | 25 | 12 |

**TABLE 2.12**

**Locus of determination for policy areas (in % of organizations) (1999)**

The UK pattern is strikingly different from the EU averages, which suggest a dominant centralized approach for all policy areas. However, as always, country differences do exist. Most notable is a southern European bloc of Italy, Portugal, Spain, and Greece that tends to centralize all or most of its policy decisions at the international and/or national levels. In contrast is a scattering of nations where decisions are more evenly distributed at centralized and decentralized locations, such as in Denmark, Finland, France, the UK and Ireland. From that group, Irish organizations are the most likely to decentralize policy making to their individual establishments or business units.

UK sectors almost mirror the two European extremes described. At one end are the sectors that are highly centralized – non-manufacturing industries, business services and other service companies. In these sectors, centralized decision making occurs for a minimum of half of all organizations. Non-manufacturing industries tend to be the most centralized, with about seven out of ten firms making policy decisions at an international or national level. At the other end are manufacturers. Here, decentralization occurs in a minimum of six out of every ten firms for all policy areas. The greatest discretion is given regarding industrial relations, with over half (51 per cent) of manufacturers determining such policy at the operational level. Surprisingly, public-sector employers are allowed considerable decentralized decision making, although not for pay policy.

In sum, UK workplaces tend to follow both centralized and decentralized approaches to policy decision making, except in the case of pay and benefits, where the majority of workplaces must take directions from headquarters.

## CONCLUSION

Despite the rhetoric, the signs show that HR functions are pretty much the same as a decade ago. It is not that HR is not taken seriously; indications towards that have always been quite positive. It is that given all the change occurring within organizations – globalization, rebranding, restructuring, downsizing, etc. – progress towards increased HR strategy has, for the most part, remained static. HR integration has still not been achieved in half of all UK workplaces, and formal HR strategies exist in only six out of every ten organizations. Less than half of employers are concerned with evaluating their HR activities to see if they work. The function also appears to be largely unfazed by other trends, excepting outsourcing. It is unclear if devolution is occurring, but quite clear that the HR function is still involved in most HR policy areas, usually as a partner with line management, unchanged over the decade. Decentralization, best practice or not, appears to occur only in policy areas where financial concerns are not paramount, and more likely in manufacturing firms. It would seem then that it is not up to the HR function to determine what to decentralize, but executive management. While there are some specific differences for each of the EU members, the overall snapshot is much the same: there are no clear leaders when it comes to HR strategy.

*"HR professionals recognize management of change as one of their top challenges for the next few years"*

These static results should act as an impetus to the HR field, particularly at the start of a new decade and a new millennium. Practitioners can expect a lot of the same broad organizational changes, and may find themselves sidelined as ineffective business partners if they continue with the status quo. HR professionals are not unaware of their situation. They recognize management of change as one of their top challenges for the next few years. Perhaps it is their own changing roles that must be most carefully managed. The Cranet data are useful benchmarks with which to track progress. Let us hope that by the time the next survey is conducted, progress is more evident.

# REFERENCES

Arkin, A. (1999) 'Return to centre', *People Management*, 5 (9), pp. 34–41.

Becker, B. & Gerhart, B. (1996) 'The impact of human resource management on organizational performance: progress and prospects', *Academy of Management Journal*, 39 (4), pp. 779–801.

Brewster, C. (1995) 'HRM: The European dimension' in J. Storey (ed.) *Human Resource Management: A critical text*. London: Routledge, pp. 309–31.

Brewster, C. & Hegewisch, A. (eds) (1994) *Policy and Practice in European Human Resource Management*. London: Routledge.

Brewster, C. & Holt Larsen, H. (1992) 'Human resource management in Europe: Evidence from ten countries', *The International Journal of Human Resource Management*, 3 (3), pp. 409–34.

Cully, M., Woodland S., O'Reilly, A. & Dix, A. (1999) *Britain at Work: As depicted by the 1998 Workplace Employee Relations Survey*. London: Routledge.

Davidson, L. (1998) 'Cut away noncore HR', *Workforce*, 77 (1), pp. 40–5.

Downie, B. & Coates, M. (1995) 'Barriers, challenges, and future directions' in B. Downie & M. Coates (eds) *Managing Human Resources in the 1990s and Beyond: Is the workplace being transformed?* Kingston, Ontario: IRC Press, Queen's University, pp. 164–85.

Griffiths, W. (2000) 'Opinion', *Personnel Today*, 1 February, p. 20.

Institute for Personnel Development (IPD). (1995) *Personnel and the Line: Developing the new relationship*. London: IPD.

Kochan, T. & Dyer, L. (1995) 'HRM: An American view' in J. Storey (ed.) *Human Resource Management: A critical text*. London: Routledge, pp. 332–51.

Pfeffer, J. (1996). 'When it comes to "best practices" – why do smart organizations occasionally do dumb things?' *Organizational Dynamics*, 25 (1), pp. 33–44.

Sisson, K. (1995) 'Human resource management and the personnel function' in J. Storey (ed.) *Human Resource Management: A critical text*. London: Routledge, pp. 87–109.

Storey, J. (1995) 'Human resource management: Still marching on, or marching out?' in J. Storey (ed.) *Human Resource Management: A critical text*. London: Routledge, pp. 3–32.

Towers-Perrin/IBM (1992) *Priorities for Competitive Advantage*. New York: Towers-Perrin.

Tyson, S. & Doherty, N. (1999) *Human Resource Excellence Report*. London: Financial Times Management.

# 3

# Recruitment and selection

## EXECUTIVE SUMMARY

- In 1999 in the UK, the majority of organizations reported recruitment difficulties, with technical/professional staff being the most problematic group to recruit. A similar situation applies across the EU, with the exception of France where managers are more difficult to recruit.

- The use of advertising, in newspapers as well as in professional journals, for managerial positions is much more common in the UK than in the rest of the EU. Countries in southern Europe tend to use less advertising at all managerial levels. The growth in internet recruitment is expected to reduce the use of traditional recruitment methods, in particular of advertising. At the moment, internet recruitment is especially used for the recruitment of graduates.

- The Cranet data strongly support the view that organizations tend to develop one standard method of staffing for different occupational groups and grades. For example, 90 per cent of organizations that generally recruit manual employees from current employees also recruit clerical employees from within.

- Whether organizations rely on internal or external recruitment depends, to a large extent, on the level of the position for which they are recruiting. Managers are recruited internally, except for senior managers. The country where the organization is located, and not the size of an organization, is the most determining factor in this process.

- In the UK organizations use the well-known combination of interviewing, application forms and references to select employees; but, with the main exception of Ireland, this way of selecting is rare in other European countries.

- Monitoring the recruitment and selection process to avoid discrimination is a key activity in the UK. The same does not apply in other European countries.

*"Organizations tend to develop one standard method of staffing for different occupational groups and grades"*

## INTRODUCTION

This chapter focuses on the staffing practices of organizations. Staffing practices are defined as all practices aiming to attract or to select job applicants. Staffing practices determine the quality and quantity of the human resources in the organization. Therefore, efficient and effective staffing is a key determinant of organizational performance. Nowadays, excellent books on personnel selection in the UK are available (e.g. Cook, 1999). In contrast, information on how organizations attract job applicants is much more limited. The focus of this chapter is therefore aimed at bridging this gap, and providing information on how organizations attract job applicants, generally referred to as recruitment.

Recruitment is essential to effective human resource management. Recruitment draws an important resource – human capital – into the organization. The effectiveness of later human resource activities, such as selection and training, depends largely on the quality of new employees attracted through the recruitment process.

Recruitment is also essential to the society as a whole. Recruitment influences job seekers' opportunities of finding suitable employment and, because work is a central part of many people's lives, those opportunities, in turn, can have a substantial impact on the applicants' well-being (Barber, 1998). Discrimination against job seekers for reason of race, gender, age, or because they belong to disadvantaged groups in society, is not desirable from a moral, legal and, sometimes, organizational point of view. Monitoring staffing practices and outcomes to avoid discrimination is, therefore, relevant to many HR managers.

Organizations have a large variety of options for attracting suitable job applicants to vacancies (the recruitment process is essentially a search process to identify and attract suitable applicants). One might anticipate that organizations use different recruitment and selection methods for different occupational groups. Although this is true to a certain extent, organizations tend to develop one standard method of recruiting that is used to attract workers from a variety of different occupational groups (*see* Cohen & Pfeffer, 1986). This justifies this chapter's approach of focusing not only on staffing practices for specific occupational groups, but also on staffing practices at the organizational level.

The chapter presents findings on:

- the extent of employers' recruitment difficulties and how to deal with these difficulties;

- how employers fill vacancies, including evidence of the extent of internal recruitment, the use of recruitment methods and selection methods;

- whether organizations monitor the position of disadvantaged groups in society, and to what extent organizations actively target those groups.

In contrast to other chapters in this report, time trends in staffing practices receive little attention, since questions in this area varied on the surveys over the decade. Hence, results generally refer to 1999, and occasionally to 1992 or 1995, the appropriate date being indicated in the text.

## RECRUITMENT DIFFICULTIES AND THE LABOUR MARKET

Staffing practices are shaped by the state of the labour market, which is characterized by the supply and demand for labour. In a tight labour market, when there are extensive recruitment difficulties and a shortage of skills and job applicants, organizations tend to recruit more intensively, using a wider range of recruitment methods. In a plentiful labour market, characterized by high unemployment and a large number of job applicants, organizations restrict the use of recruitment methods and intensify the use of pre-screening and selection (Russo & van Ommeren, 1998). Further, organizations that are expanding have more difficulties attracting staff (RCI, 2000a).

In the UK in 1999 the unemployment rate was lower and levels of vacancies were higher than they had been for nearly two decades. In contrast, in 1992 and 1995 the economy was less buoyant. Other European countries exhibit different patterns. For example, in Germany in 1999 the labour market was characterized by historically high unemployment levels, whereas in the Netherlands and Ireland the labour market was extremely tight.

Levels of labour supply and demand are the main determinant of the proportion of organizations with recruitment difficulties. Considering the UK's low unemployment and high vacancy levels, in 1999, most organizations (83 per cent) reported recruitment difficulties. However, difficulties are usually restricted to a few occupational groups. Distinguishing between five broad occupational groups (management, professional/technical, IT, clerical, manual), only 12 per cent of organizations reported difficulties for more than two groups, and 1 per cent for all five groups.

Considerable differences between occupational groups in the perception of recruitment difficulties exist (*see* Table 3.1). Overall, 20 per cent of organizations mentioned difficulties in recruiting managers, considerably less than the 42 per cent that mentioned difficulties in recruiting professional/technical staff. Recruitment difficulties for clerical and manual employees were less common (10 and 15 per cent respectively). The overall impression is that in the UK recruitment difficulties are widespread, but are in particular present when organizations are looking for specific professional/technical skills. Only a few organizations had problems attracting employees for a wide range of occupational groups.

**TABLE 3.1**

Recruitment difficulties by occupation and sector (in % of organizations)

| | UK 1999 Manufac- turing | Other industry | Business services | Other services | Public sector | UK average | EU 1999 EU average |
|---|---|---|---|---|---|---|---|
| Management | 26 | 21 | 16 | 25 | 9 | 20 | 34 |
| Professional/ technical | 46 | 45 | 44 | 38 | 40 | 42 | 36 |
| IT | 49 | 54 | 63 | 46 | 63 | 54 | 46 |
| Clerical | 9 | 9 | 22 | 13 | 5 | 10 | 8 |
| Manual | 22 | 16 | 0 | 20 | 9 | 15 | 18 |

In the public sector, difficulties are less common, in particular for managerial staff (*see* Table 3.1). Less than one out of ten public-sector organizations (9 per cent) had difficulties attracting managerial staff. In manufacturing, respondents are more likely to report recruitment difficulties for management than in business services, which may be related to the pessimistic long-term perspectives of the manufacturing sector, which reduce career opportunities for management.

*"Recruitment difficulties are widespread, but are in particular present when organizations are looking for specific professional/technical skills"*

Compared to the EU average, organizations in the UK were slightly more likely to experience recruitment difficulties (83 per cent compared to 74 per cent). However, the EU average hides widely varying country differences. In France and, in particular, Finland, organizations have relatively fewer problems attracting staff (in Finland, although 53 per cent of organizations reported difficulties, only 4 per cent reported difficulties for at least three occupational groups), whereas in Ireland, Belgium and the Netherlands the problems are more widespread. (In Ireland 89 per cent reported difficulties and 32 per cent reported difficulties for at least three occupational groups.) In the latter countries, organizations experience much higher levels of recruitment difficulty for all job categories than in the UK. For example, 31 per cent of organizations in the Netherlands, compared to 15 per cent in the UK, reported recruitment difficulties for manual employees.

Compared to the EU average, organizations in the UK are less likely to experience difficulties in recruiting managerial staff, but more likely to experience them in recruiting professional/technical employees. In particular, attracting IT specialists is problematic in the UK: only 46 per cent of organizations in the EU had difficulties attracting IT specialists, compared to 54 per cent in the UK (*see* Table 3.1). Patterns in occupational differences in recruitment difficulties are comparable across Europe. But there are also exceptions. For example, in France attracting managers is considerably more difficult than attracting professional/technical staff: about half the organizations had difficulties attracting managers, and only one in four organizations had difficulty attracting professional/technical staff. The main explanation for this is that in France managers are expected to have a degree from specific institutes (*grandes écoles*), which restricts the pool of applicants, but in other European countries the required background is less specific.

## Solutions to recruitment difficulties

When confronted with recruitment difficulties, or when these difficulties are expected, organizations usually undertake a wide range of actions, of which the most popular ones are discussed briefly here:

- increasing compensation levels
- retraining existing employees
- marketing the organization's image
- relocating
- recruiting abroad.

As can be seen from Table 3.2, the variation in the use of these actions is small between 1995 and 1999, with the exception of pay increases.

| | UK 1995 | 1999 | EU 1999 |
|---|---|---|---|
| Increasing pay/benefits | 41 | 55 | 41 |
| Retraining employees | 63 | 54 | 50 |
| Marketing of image | 28 | 33 | 38 |
| Relocation | 6 | 5 | 7 |
| Recruiting abroad | 15 | 16 | 16 |

**TABLE 3.2**

**Actions related to recruitment (in % of organizations)**

### Increasing compensation levels

One of the most common ways to deal with recruitment differently is pay. In the UK in 1999 55 per cent of organizations increased compensation levels in relation to recruitment/retention, particularly in services (business services: 72 per cent; other services: 64 per cent). In the public sector such increase in compensation levels was less common (35 per cent) (*see* Table 3.3). Strong pay increases in the service sector have also been observed elsewhere (RCI, 2000c). The data indicate that increasing compensation levels has become more common in the second half of the 1990s.

**TABLE 3.3**

**Actions related to recruitment by sector (in % of organizations)**

|  | UK 1999 Manufacturing | Other industry | Business services | Other services | Public sector |
|---|---|---|---|---|---|
| Increasing pay/benefits | 52 | 54 | 72 | 64 | 35 |
| Retraining employees | 62 | 43 | 48 | 53 | 48 |
| Marketing of image | 28 | 34 | 41 | 42 | 28 |
| Relocation | 8 | 5 | 6 | 3 | 3 |
| Recruiting abroad | 15 | 7 | 26 | 15 | 17 |

Increasing compensation is, on average, more popular in the UK than in the rest of Europe, where collective bargaining, which restricts pay flexibility, is more common. Even in countries such as the Netherlands, where recruitment difficulties are more widespread, increasing compensation levels is less common.

### Retraining existing employees

Another option is to retrain employees in needed skills. More than half of UK organizations (54 per cent) retrained employees, particularly in manufacturing (62 per cent), roughly comparable to the European average (50 per cent). In the Netherlands, Sweden, Germany and Spain, retraining is more frequently used, possibly because organizations have less freedom to increase compensation levels.

### Marketing the organization's image

Organizations with a good reputation attract more unsolicited applications than other organizations. Further, these organizations are also more likely to attract applicants when using advertising or recruitment agencies. Hence, to attract applicants, 33 per cent of organizations in the UK actively marketed their image (*see* Table 3.2). This is about the same as for the rest of the EU (38 per cent). The variation among European countries is small in this respect, although countries in southern Europe tend to use marketing less often for recruitment.

### Relocating

Organizations may relocate to regions with a larger supply of applicants, but this is not so common. In 1999 only 5 per cent of UK organizations reported having relocated the organization, the most common being in manufacturing (8 per cent). In geographically smaller countries, relocation occurs even less often. For example, only 3 per cent of organizations in Ireland have relocated the organization in relation to recruitment. In France relocation is more common (14 per cent) than in the EU on average (7 per cent).

### Recruiting abroad

Lastly, organizations may broaden their search by recruiting from abroad. Of the UK employees 16 per cent stated having recruited from abroad, and more so in business services (26 per cent). In smaller countries recruiting abroad is more common. For example, in Ireland recruiting from abroad is the norm (44 per cent) – a remarkable reversal from only a few years ago when Ireland was a primary recruitment target for many other countries.

## The response to recruitment difficulties

The greater the recruitment difficulties the more likely organizations are to turn to pay increases, retraining and international recruitment (*see* Table 3.4). This is perhaps to be expected. Yet it does not indicate high levels of proactive behaviour: organizations tend to wait until they face problems before they seriously move to redress them.

| | UK 1999 No recruitment difficulties | Recruitment difficulties for one occupational group | Recruitment difficulties for two occupational groups | Recruitment difficulties for at least three occupational groups |
|---|---|---|---|---|
| Increasing pay/benefits | 30 | 57 | 62 | 62 |
| Retraining employees | 47 | 51 | 55 | 68 |
| Marketing of image | 26 | 32 | 35 | 45 |
| Relocation | 4 | 5 | 6 | 5 |
| Recruiting abroad | 13 | 15 | 18 | 23 |

**TABLE 3.4**

**Actions related to recruitment by recruitment difficulties (in % of organizations)**

## HOW EMPLOYERS ATTRACT APPLICANTS

After a vacancy has been identified, employers attract suitable applicants by going through a number of steps, of which the following are discussed in detail here:

- whether to recruit internally or externally

- the choice of recruitment methods (formal, informal, the internet).

### Internal v. external recruitment

One of the most fundamental questions when looking for staff is whether to recruit internally or externally. Labour markets within organizations operate very differently to external labour markets. The external labour market is determined by the supply and demand for labour, whereas rules and procedures largely determine the internal labour markets of organizations. Internal labour markets tend to be most developed in large organizations with specific job ladders, with entry only at the bottom. Movement up this ladder is associated with seniority and progressive development of knowledge and skill. Most organizations do not have such a developed internal labour market, and recruit externally at all employee levels, including managerial levels.

*"Organizations where internal recruitment is common are less responsive to changes in the external environment"*

Internal recruitment has several advantages. Recruiting from within is cheaper. Also, the organization already has much information available about the applicant's behaviour and job performance. Further, it offers promotion and development opportunities for staff, which create incentives for staff to do well. It also reduces the induction time taken to become familiar with the organization's procedures. The latter is particularly important in large organizations, since these organizations are so complex that knowledge about the organization may be as important as job-specific knowledge. However, relying on internal recruitment has some risks, as there are reduced opportunities to benefit from the experiences of employees who have worked in other organizations. Organizations where internal recruitment is common are plausibly less responsive to changes in the external environment.

#### Occupational differences

Whether organizations rely mainly on internal or external recruitment depends to a large extent on the level of the position for which they are recruiting. This issue is investigated using 1992 data distinguishing between managerial, professional/technical, clerical and manual employees. In the UK 75 per cent of organizations recruited managers internally, whereas this figure is much lower for other occupations (professional/technical: 54 per cent; clerical: 57 per cent; manual: 36 per cent). It seems that the internal labour market is more important for the recruitment of managers than for other occupational groups.

### Managerial differences

There is one exception to the predominance of internal promotion to management. Senior management positions are less often filled internally than managerial positions lower in the hierarchy (*see* Table 3.5). Apparently, for many senior management positions, external applicants are, or are perceived to be, better qualified than those from inside the organization. This suggests that in order to take strategic decisions, managerial experience within the organization is sometimes less important than experience outside the organization. This may have many reasons. For example, external applicants may have become familiar with organizational changes that are needed. Another reason is that experience within the organization may be detrimental due to involvement in the politics of the organization, which reduces opportunities to deliver needed change.

| | UK 1995 | 1999 | EU 1999 |
|---|---|---|---|
| Senior | 65 | 57 | 55 |
| Middle | 82 | 77 | 76 |
| Junior | 87 | 75 | 68 |

**TABLE 3.5**

**Internal recruitment by management level (in % of organizations)**

Internal recruitment has advantages when organizations wish to become more flexible (in terms of structure and size). This numerical flexibility may be a good response to changing external environments. In line with the popular view that numerical flexibility has become more important, as we discuss later in this report, managerial positions were somewhat less often internally filled in 1999 than they were in 1995 (*see* Table 3.5), suggesting that the internal labour markets of large organizations are opening up further and the external influence on the managerial internal labour markets of organizations is increasing.

The type of sector in which the organization operates is not very relevant in this respect. The main exception is that public-sector organizations tend to fill their managerial vacancies externally, which is not in agreement with common wisdom (*see* Table 3.6). Larger organizations have access to a larger pool of suitable internal applicants for managerial positions than smaller organizations. However, this advantage materializes only for organizations with at least 5000 employees. Of organizations with less than 5000 employees, 60 per cent generally filled their senior managerial positions internally, compared to 80 per cent of organizations with more than 5000 employees.

**TABLE 3.6**

**Internal recruitment by management level and sector (in % of organizations)**

| | UK 1999 Manufac- turing | Other industry | Business services | Other services | Public sector | UK average | EU 1999 EU average |
|---|---|---|---|---|---|---|---|
| Senior management | 51 | 79 | 61 | 59 | 51 | 57 | 52 |
| Middle management | 80 | 91 | 74 | 83 | 64 | 77 | 76 |
| Junior management | 77 | 73 | 75 | 82 | 65 | 75 | 62 |

Perhaps surprisingly, the national environment has only a small effect on the decision to recruit senior, or middle, management from within (EU: 52 and 76 per cent, respectively). The main exception is that internal recruitment of senior management in Scandinavian countries is less common, in particular in Denmark (around 30 per cent of organizations). UK organizations recruited marginally more from within, since UK organizations tend to be larger than in the rest of the EU.

The decision to recruit junior management is far more strongly influenced by the national environment. In most of Europe, including the UK, junior management is usually recruited from within (in the EU 62 per cent generally recruit from within). However, in contrast, in southern Europe junior management is less often recruited internally (Spain: 44 per cent; France: 29 per cent). So it seems that in southern Europe the internal labour markets of organizations are less developed than elsewhere in Europe. In the rest of Europe, employees that are recruited at the bottom of the job ladder have some opportunity to reach a managerial level, whereas in southern Europe these opportunities are scarcer. The main explanation is that, particularly in France, junior management is expected to have a specific educational background, while work experience is of less importance.

## Recruitment methods

The decision to look for staff internally or externally is usually followed by the choice of a recruitment method. The type of recruitment method strongly influences the number and type of job applicants (Russo, 1996). The success of a method in generating a sufficient number of suitable applicants depends on the effective use of hiring criteria that are announced to job seekers (e.g. requirements of experience, education, age, etc.). When the hiring criteria are stated inappropriately, either too many or too few applicants will emerge. Since screening and selection are expensive and labour intensive, strict hiring criteria should be used when many applicants are expected, in order to narrow the number of applicants to manageable proportions. Thus the problem facing the employer is not to contact the largest possible number of potential applicants; rather it is to find a sufficient number of applicants who are promising enough to be worth investing in a thorough selection process. This problem is particularly relevant to organizations that have recently started to use the internet for recruitment and are overloaded with less suitable applicants.

Organizations sometimes use a range of recruitment methods for the same vacancy, especially for managerial positions. This is not necessarily simultaneous. So an important aspect of the recruitment process is how employers combine the use of a range of recruitment methods. Several strategies have been identified (Gorter & van Ommeren, 1999). One is to advertise a vacancy and to form a pool of candidates while subsequently activating recruitment methods adding candidates to the pool. So the new employee is the best applicant chosen from a pool of applicants. Larger organizations tend to prefer this strategy. An alternative strategy used by employers is to start searching via word of mouth, consider applicants at arrival and continue their search along a new recruitment method if no suitable candidates turn up. So applicants are not selected from a pool of applicants, but are screened subsequently until an acceptable applicant becomes available. Where informal personal contacts are available to the employer, this 'switching' of recruitment method strategy is preferred, since the use of personal contacts is more cost-effective than using an advertisement. If an informal search turns out to be unsuccessful, employers can quickly switch to other recruitment methods, such as advertisements.

Recruitment methods are usually classified into two broad classes: formal and informal. Formal recruitment methods make use of some intermediary, such as recruitment agencies, commercial job websites and advertisements.

Informal recruitment methods are based on a search via informal contacts and are essentially word of mouth. The use of corporate job websites and unsolicited applications do not fit easily in this categorisation.

### Informal recruitment methods

Informal recruitment relies on referrals and therefore on a referral network of colleagues, friends and family. Social networks are important for recruitment because job-related information flows through a network of friends and relatives, and only reaches a selected group of seekers. These networks are, however, not only used to pass information about job openings, they also pass information on about organizations to job seekers, and information about job seekers to organizations. So organizations consider the use of informal recruitment to be inexpensive and effective, because job-related information conveyed in this way is reliable. This may explain why some studies reported that staff turnover of employees recruited via informal recruitment methods is substantially lower. Other studies challenge this finding. Currently there is no agreement among academics how employee performance is related to recruitment method.

*"Positions that require specific knowledge, skills and experience are less often filled using informal recruitment"*

Informal recruitment reaches relatively few job seekers and is therefore not well suited to recruiting over a broad geographic region. As a result, commuting distances of employees recruited via informal recruitment methods are substantially smaller than those recruited via formal recruitment methods (Russo, 1996). This has some advantages: for example, employees with short commuting distances are less likely to search for other jobs and are less likely to quit (van Ommeren, 2000). Furthermore, in as far as most workforces are quite homogenous, informal recruitment is likely to replicate the existing workforce so it might be indirectly discriminatory.

Informal methods, by relying on contacts of existing employees or on people just getting in touch, tend to generate a smaller pool of potential applicants. This is less of a disadvantage when the knowledge, skills and experience required for a position are less specific. Positions that require specific knowledge, skills and experience, such as professional/technical and managerial occupations, are less often filled using informal recruitment (*see* Table 3.7). In 1992 38 per cent of organizations generally used word of mouth to attract manual employees and 30 per cent to attract clerical employees (1999 data not available).

| | UK 1992 Advertise externally | Word of mouth | Recruitment agencies | Search/ selection consultancies |
|---|---|---|---|---|
| Management | 78 | 11 | 43 | 50 |
| Professional | 87 | 14 | 53 | 24 |
| Clerical | 76 | 30 | 39 | 1 |
| Manual | 63 | 38 | 9 | 1 |

**TABLE 3.7**

**Methods generally used to fill vacancies, by occupation (in % of organizations)**

This does not mean that informal recruitment is unknown at the top of organizations. In 1999 14 per cent of organizations generally used word of mouth to fill positions at senior management level. At middle and junior management levels, 16 and 22 per cent respectively, generally used word of mouth. These figures are comparable to 1995.

Due to its image of being indirectly discriminatory, word-of-mouth recruitment is hardly acceptable in the public sector. In contrast, in the business services sector, word-of-mouth recruitment is common. One reason might be that in this sector, due to the nature of their work, employees have larger social networks.

Word-of-mouth recruitment for managerial positions is not systematically less popular in the UK, which is a bit surprising given the emphasis in the UK on fair recruitment practices (*see* Table 3.8). International differences in the use of informal recruitment at managerial levels are substantial, but, maybe surprisingly, the data do not support the belief that informal recruitment is more popular in southern Europe. Word-of-mouth recruitment of senior, middle and junior management is popular in Sweden (25, 28 and 31 per cent respectively) and Spain (25, 26 and 29 per cent respectively), but not in Italy (7, 10 and 16 per cent respectively) or Portugal (13, 16 and 12 per cent respectively). Currently, more research is needed to explain international variation in the use of recruitment methods.

| | UK 1999 Manufac- turing | Other industry | Business services | Other services | Public sector | UK average | EU 1999 EU average |
|---|---|---|---|---|---|---|---|
| Senior management | 11 | 16 | 28 | 17 | 4 | 14 | 11 |
| Middle management | 13 | 18 | 40 | 20 | 3 | 16 | 17 |
| Junior management | 23 | 32 | 45 | 25 | 4 | 22 | 24 |

**TABLE 3.8**

**Word-of-mouth recruitment by management level and sector (in % of organizations)**

### Formal recruitment methods

Formal recruitment methods, although generally more expensive than informal ones, usually generate a much larger number of applicants from more diverse social groups. This can involve considerable screening activities, in that such methods may generate large, rather undifferentiated pools of applicants. This is particularly true for the use of advertisements and internet recruitment. Human-resource textbooks tend to overemphasize the advantages of the use of advertising, suggesting that creating a (large) pool of applicants is best practice. In contrast, as argued above, in many cases, informal recruitment is more effective.

Occupational differences in the use of advertising are small (*see* Table 3.7). In 1999 about 70 per cent of organizations in the UK used advertising in newspapers to attract middle and junior managers, whereas 55 per cent of organizations used this medium to attract senior managers. In particular, for the public sector, with its ethos of openness and anti-discrimination, the use of advertising in newspapers is popular (87 per cent). Otherwise, sectoral differences are small.

National differences in the use of advertising are large. In the UK advertising in newspapers is much more common than in the rest of the EU for senior, middle and junior management positions (UK: 56, 74, 72 per cent; EU: 23, 51, 51 per cent). Countries in southern Europe tend to use less advertising at all managerial levels. National differences in the use of professional journals for managerial positions are also large. In the UK particularly, the use of professional journals is common, which reflects the number of professional journals in the national market. By contrast, in Ireland, the use of professional journals is rare, due to the scarcity of national country-specific professional journals.

Recruitment agencies are rarely used for manual employees, and the use of expensive search and selection consultancies is limited to managers and professional/technical staff (*see* Table 3.7). In most European countries headhunters and selection agencies are more often used to attract senior management than any other method. For example, in the UK in 1999, 65 per cent of organizations used these agencies to attract senior management (EU: 58 per cent). In contrast, 40 per cent used them to attract middle management (EU: 34 per cent) and 21 per cent to attract junior management (EU: 18 per cent). In southern Europe organizations tend to use a smaller range of recruitment methods than in the rest of Europe; the reasons for this are unknown.

### Internet recruitment

The recruitment market is continuously changing. The most important recent development is the growth in internet recruitment. When the latest Cranet Survey was developed, internet recruitment was still in its infancy and was not covered by the survey. Thus research by Cranfield School of Management in conjunction with *The Daily Telegraph* and TMP Worldwide in this area will be discussed (RCI, 2000a; RCI, 2000b; RCI, 2000c).

In March 2000 37 per cent of organizations made use of internet recruitment (RCI, 2000c). In particular, the growth in the use of commercial job websites has been phenomenal. About 56 per cent of respondents expected to increase the use of internet recruitment within a year. In March 2000 more than 20 per cent of organizations expected to reduce the use of traditional recruitment methods within a year due to the take up of internet recruitment (RCI, 2000c). In particular, employment agencies and newspapers are to be used less due to this increase. However, recruitment agencies that resource mainly at higher managerial/professional levels (selection consultants, executive search agencies) would be affected to a lesser extent. Internet recruitment is generally limited to a small number of occupational levels.

Currently, distinguishing between six employee levels, about 40 per cent of organizations use the internet for only one employee level (mainly graduate). Only a minority of organizations use the internet for a wide range of employee levels. For organizations that use a commercial website for recruitment, but not their corporate website, the extent of its use is even more limited.

Focusing at managerial/professional level, organizations' use of internet recruitment strongly decreases with the level of appointment. For example, 37 per cent of organizations that recruit at graduate level have used internet recruitment, in contrast to 22 per cent that recruit at senior level.

## Standard methods of staffing

In the introduction it was emphasized that organizations tend to develop one standard method of staffing for different occupational groups and grades. The Cranet data strongly support this view. Indeed, it can be shown that if manual employees are generally recruited internally, other types of employees are likely to be as well (*see* Table 3.9): 90 per cent of organizations that generally recruit manual employees from current employees also recruit clerical employees from within (1992 data).

**TABLE 3.9**

**Internal recruitment by occupation (in % of organizations) depending on whether manual employees are generally internally recruited**

| Internal recruitment | UK 1992 Manual employees: internally recruited? | |
| --- | --- | --- |
| | Yes | No |
| Management | 81 | 71 |
| Professional | 71 | 45 |
| Clerical | 90 | 39 |

Focusing on management levels, we observe the same phenomenon. Organizations that generally recruit senior management internally also, generally, recruit middle and junior management from within (94 and 82 per cent respectively), whereas other organizations are less likely to recruit lower management levels from within (57 and 65 per cent respectively).

Another way of presenting these data is by categorizing organizations according to what extent they use internal recruitment at management level. Almost half of organizations (46 per cent) generally recruit internally at all management levels, 43 per cent recruit internally at one or two management levels, whereas 11 per cent of organizations generally do not recruit internally at any management level.

The same can be said for different management recruitment methods (*see* Table 3.10, based on 1992 data). When external advertising is used to fill managerial vacancies, 95 per cent of organizations use the same method to recruit professional/technical staff. Of organizations that generally do not use advertising to attract managers, only 58 per cent use advertising to attract professional/technical staff. When managerial vacancies are generally filled without using word of mouth, only 7 per cent of organizations use word of mouth to recruit professional/technical staff.

**TABLE 3.10**

**Methods used to fill vacancies by occupation (in % of organizations) depending on how managerial vacancies are generally filled**

| | UK 1992 Management: advertise externally? | | Management: word of mouth? | |
| --- | --- | --- | --- | --- |
| | Yes | No | Yes | No |
| Professional | 95 | 58 | 76 | 7 |
| Clerical | 82 | 51 | 73 | 24 |
| Manual | 68 | 47 | 60 | 35 |

So, the overall conclusion is that organizations tend to use the same staffing methods for different occupations and grades. As indicated by other research, the choice of the staffing method depends on the organizational environment (Cohen & Pfeffer, 1986). This indicates that the organizational environment is relevant to recruitment, an aspect often ignored.

## SELECTION METHODS

After a job applicant has reacted to the announcement of a vacancy, the organization has to make the decision whether or not to accept this applicant for the vacancy. Selection involves the identification of the most suitable person from a pool of applicants. Organizations can choose from a wide range of selection methods. Occupational psychologists claim that choosing more trustworthy, but more expensive, selection methods is best practice. 'The most important property of the selection method is its predictive validity: the ability to predict future job performance, job-related learning (such as amount of learning in training and development programmes), and other criteria' (Schmidt & Hunter, 1998).

*"The combination of selection methods guarantees a higher overall predictive validity"*

Extensive work by psychologists since the first decade of the 20th century has demonstrated that the validity of some selection methods is reasonably high, whereas other methods have no predictive value whatsoever. In particular, the validity of some psychometric testing methods (i.e. general mental-ability tests) is undisputed, whereas the validity of using the applicants' general interests (e.g. leisure activities) is zero or close to zero. Remarkably, psychologists claim that the variability of validity across settings for the same type of job and across different kinds of jobs is small (Schmidt & Hunter, 1998). Nevertheless, some variation is observed, in particular the validity of psychometric testing is much higher for managerial/professional jobs than for unskilled jobs. This is relevant since screening and selection of job applicants is particularly appropriate for managerial and professional positions, because the variation in job applicants' qualities is large for jobs requiring higher skill levels. The combination of selection methods guarantees a higher overall predictive validity. Therefore it is often wise not to use one type of selection method, but a range of selection methods.

In the UK, interviews (either interview panels or one-to-one interviews), standard application forms and references are commonly used as part of the recruitment and selection process. For most appointments, 96 per cent of organizations use employment interviews, 84 per cent use application forms and 91 per cent use references. In fact, 43 per cent of organizations in the UK use a combination of interviews, standard application forms and references for every appointment (*see* Table 3.11). For the rest of Europe, with the exception of Ireland, a different picture emerges. Application forms, but also the use of references, are less popular (66 and 34 per cent respectively). Another difference is that in the UK, interview panels, which are thought to have higher predictive validity than one-to-one interviews, are much more common than in the rest of Europe.

**TABLE 3.11**

**Selection methods used for most or all appointments (in % of organizations)**

| | UK 1995 | 1999 | EU 1999 |
|---|---|---|---|
| Interviews panel | 46 | 51 | 38 |
| One-to-one interviews | 47 | 55 | 79 |
| References | 87 | 89 | 44 |
| Application forms | 87 | 82 | 68 |
| Psychometric test | 15 | 16 | 16 |
| Assessment centre | 3 | 7 | 6 |
| Graphology | 1 | 0 | 4 |

Sectoral differences in the use of selection methods are small (*see* Table 3.12). In the public sector, interview panels are the norm (97 per cent for most applications). In business services, the use of interview panels and application forms is less commonly used, indicating a less formal approach to selection (a similar finding holds for the choice of recruitment methods).

**TABLE 3.12**

**Selection methods used for most appointments by sector (in % of organizations)**

| | UK 1999 Manufacturing | Other industry | Business services | Other services | Public sector |
|---|---|---|---|---|---|
| Interview panel | 33 | 36 | 24 | 46 | 97 |
| One-to-one interview | 79 | 80 | 86 | 67 | 10 |
| References | 80 | 93 | 91 | 96 | 97 |
| Application forms | 81 | 82 | 61 | 89 | 87 |
| Psychometric tests | 24 | 16 | 23 | 20 | 34 |
| Assessment centre | 7 | 7 | 4 | 10 | 5 |

In Europe, including the UK, but in contrast to the USA, interviews are generally unstructured, despite unstructured interviews having low predictive validity. Nevertheless, HR managers, worried about the low predictive validity of interviewing, would not be advised to discontinue this activity completely, since the interview is still very useful to convey information to the candidates about the vacancy/organization. Better advice would be to structure the interview, thus increasing its validity (Cook, 1999).

Only a small minority of organizations (16 per cent for most appointments) use psychometric testing and the proportion of organizations that use assessment centres is even smaller (7 per cent for most appointments). In this respect, UK organizations are not much different from the European average (20 and 5 per cent, respectively). Again, differences between countries are large. For example, in Sweden assessment centres are hardly used (1 per cent for most appointments). In Spain 48 per cent of organizations use psychometric testing for most appointments, in the Netherlands only 6 per cent.

If there is one area in HRM where national differences are apparent, it is in the area of selection. Some selection methods are common in some countries, but may not be used at all in others (e.g. graphology is relatively popular in France – 17 per cent use graphology for most appointments – and in some parts of Switzerland, but is hardly used elsewhere). One of the reasons why selection methods are diverse among countries is plausibly that some selection methods have a low predictive validity. This does not mean that the choice of the selection method is arbitrary, but it means that the perceived economic costs of not using the optimal selection methods are relatively small. From this perspective it is very plausible that national differences in selection methods are mainly related to national differences in social norms and culture. Nevertheless, it may be expected that selection methods that have been shown to have poor reliability and validity will be replaced in the future by more trustworthy methods such as structured interviewing and psychometric testing, particularly in large organizations.

Much of what is currently known about selection is based on research and perceptions during periods of few recruitment difficulties and high unemployment. It should not be forgotten that the lessons learned from past research and experiences may be of limited application during periods of severe skill shortages and high labour turnover. Examples can easily be given, one being that the common recommendation by recruitment specialists that organizations may increase their performance by using more trustworthy, but more expensive, selection methods such as assessment centres may be invalid during periods of high labour turnover. Another example relates to standard application forms, ubiquitously used in the UK, because they simplify the selection process. Nevertheless, the standard application form may prevent job seekers from applying, as most job seekers prefer sending an individual letter and CV. Essentially, the standard is to be avoided when few job applicants are expected.

## MONITORING AND TARGETING OF DISADVANTAGED GROUPS

HR policy and practices, including staffing practices, are influenced by national and EU employment laws that restrict direct, and sometimes indirect, discrimination based on gender, race, colour, disability, religion and marital status. Regulating staffing practices can be justified on the grounds that these practices have not only major consequences for employers, but also for job seekers, and, therefore, for society at large. In the UK, relative to other countries, in particular the USA, there are few legal constraints in the area of recruitment and selection. It does not matter, according to the law, whether there is intention to discriminate. It is unlawful if the effect is to discriminate. Nevertheless, the legality of selection (and recruitment) methods is hard to evaluate, as the legal position of these methods is obscure or confused (Cook, 1999).

In the UK large organizations' selection and recruitment practices are influenced by the Commission for Racial Equality's Code and the Code of Practice issued by the Equal Opportunities Commission. These codes of conduct are short documents and do not give detailed instructions about selection and recruitment (Cook, 1999). The main recommendation is that selection criteria and tests must be examined to ensure that they are related to job requirements and are not unlawfully discriminatory. These codes also recommend monitoring and targeting of disadvantaged groups (in the workforce and in the applicant pool).

Compared to the rest of Europe, HR managers in the UK are more active in monitoring the position of disadvantaged groups (women, people with disabilities, ethnic minorities). For example, the majority of organizations in the UK monitor the proportion of women in their workforce with regard to recruitment (1992: 53 per cent, 1995: 60 per cent, 1999: 54 per cent). Approximately the same percentage of organizations monitor the proportion of people with disabilities and the proportion of ethnic minorities. By comparison, in all other European countries (with the exception of the Netherlands and Sweden) only a minority of organizations monitor the proportion of women. In particular in Italy, Spain, Denmark and Belgium, less than one in four organizations monitor the proportion of women.

Considering that amount of monitoring, it may seem unusual that HR managers in the UK are, on average, less active in targeting women in the recruitment process than in the rest of the EU. In fact, in the UK, a continuously decreasing minority of organizations actively target women in their recruitment process (1992: 32 per cent, 1995: 21 per cent, 1999: 17 per cent). In the rest of Europe a similar trend can be observed. Not surprisingly, organizations with larger proportions of female employees are much more likely to monitor the proportion of female employees and to target females in the recruitment process than those organizations with fewer female employees.

Staffing practices are also strongly influenced by norms and values that are not covered by the law. For example, most European countries – including the UK – do not outlaw discrimination on the grounds of age, but only in the UK is the use of age restriction rare. In 1995 in the UK only 5 per cent of the respondents to the Cranet Survey stated that they did not recruit people over 50. In contrast, in the Netherlands, Belgium, Germany, Spain, Italy and France more than 40 per cent of the respondents stated that they do not recruit people over 50. In most European countries age restrictions are publicly used. For example, in the Netherlands (where about 20 per cent of all vacancies have explicit age restrictions), job advertisements that contain explicit age restrictions can be seen in newspapers, on billboards etc.

## CONCLUSION

Organizational resourcing – getting the right people into the right jobs – has always been an important success factor for human resource management. The shift towards the information society and knowledge-based work has highlighted even further the strategic importance of effective recruitment and selection policies. In the context of considerable labour market shortages – the vast majority of organizations in the UK or, indeed, the whole EU, is currently reporting recruitment difficulties – recruitment and selection policies have an even greater potential impact on organizational success.

*"Even the best recruitment and selection procedures will not be able to overcome fundamental skill shortages"*

The survey shows that organizations have widened the channels they are using to try to identify and attract future employees, as would be expected in times of labour market shortages. They are also retaining employees and increasing compensation in the battle for winning the best staff. Against the background of much discussion on recruitment and selection 'good practice', organizational history – based on the sector in which an organization operates and the traditional way of doing things – appears to predominate in deciding practices in this area. Thus rather than differentiating recruitment and selection processes between groups of employees – choosing different methods for recruiting professional or clerical posts – there seems to be a set of preferred practices applied across grades. Traditional practices, interviews in particular, tend to predominate. The regular use of psychometric testing remains very much a minority occurrence in the UK.

Recruitment and above all selection practices show much evidence of national diversity. Different emphases are placed on the use of internal or external and informal or formal recruitment activities, offering varying advantages and disadvantages with each approach. This is also being complicated by the addition of a new and very powerful media, the internet, which is still in its infancy in terms of the effect which it is expected to have on recruitment and selection practices as a whole.

One issue which differentiates the UK in particular, is a much greater attention to the potentially discriminatory effect of recruitment. A history of detailed sex discrimination legislation in the UK – and a broader focus on equality of opportunity – appear to have a knock-on effect in making organizations more careful in their selection processes in general.

However, even the best recruitment and selection procedures will not be able to overcome fundamental skill shortages. And this is where the comparative disadvantage of UK organizations lies. Inadequate training and development in the past have exacerbated recruitment difficulties and have forced relatively more UK organizations to increase pay and benefits in competition for employees. Without a strategic macro and micro level approach, there is a danger of organizations being caught in this spiral of wage competition.

## REFERENCES

Barber, A.E. (1998) *Recruiting Employees*. London: Sage Publications.

Cohen, M. & Pfeffer, J. (1986) 'Organisational hiring standards', *Administrative Science Quarterly*, 31, pp. 1–24.

Cook, M. (1999) *Personnel Selection: Adding Value Through People*. Chichester: John Wiley.

Gorter, C. & van Ommeren, J.N. (1999) 'Sequencing, timing and filling rates of recruitment channels', *Applied Economics*, 31, pp. 1149–60.

RCI (2000a), *Recruitment Confidence Index January Executive Report*. Cranfield School of Management, in conjunction with *The Daily Telegraph* and TMP Worldwide.

RCI (2000b), *Recruitment Confidence Index April Executive Report*. Cranfield School of Management, in conjunction with *The Daily Telegraph* and TMP Worldwide.

RCI (2000c), *Recruitment Confidence Index Internet Recruitment Report*. Cranfield School of Management, in conjunction with *The Daily Telegraph* and TMP Worldwide.

Russo, G. (1996) *Firms' Recruitment Behaviour*, Tinbergen Institute Research Series, 129.

Russo, G. & van Ommeren, J.N. (1998) 'Gender differences in recruitment outcomes', *Bulletin of Economic Research*, 50 (2), pp. 155–66.

Schmidt, F.L. & Hunter J.E. (1998) 'The validity and utility of selection methods in personnel psychology: practical and theoretical implications of 85 years of research findings', *Psychological Bulletin*, 124 (2), pp. 262–74.

Van Ommeren, J.N. (2000) *Commuting and Relocation of Jobs and Residences*. Aldershot: Ashgate.

Van Ommeren, J.N. & Russo G. (1997) 'Are vacancies difficult to fill?', *Applied Economics*, 29, pp. 349–57.

# 4

# Flexibility and new working practices

## EXECUTIVE SUMMARY

- The findings on time and contract flexibility are mixed: few organizations report a decrease in flexible working patterns and, particularly for part-time and non-permanent employment, a consistent majority of organizations report a growth in use. Yet in the large majority of organizations permanent full-time 'standard' employment remains the norm.

- In other European countries the overall trend is towards greater time and contract flexibility. There are, however, huge differences in the type and extent of change. The Netherlands is the country that has seen most change in the greatest variety of flexible working patterns.

- Public-sector employers clearly lead the way in relation to employee-led flexible working – they are twice as likely as other employers to have job-sharing or flexitime schemes. Within Europe, the UK, apart from Greece, is the country with the lowest growth in flexitime. Flexitime schemes, clearly are not dead but neither are they a very dynamic element of change. On the other hand, twice as many UK organizations as elsewhere in Europe have job-share schemes, and twice as many have increased the use of job sharing.

- Home-based working is finally taking off, with the share of UK organizations reporting increases almost doubling since 1995. Teleworking remains sluggish. Yet developments in the UK are dwarfed by the much more widespread introduction of home-based working and teleworking in the Nordic countries, particularly in Sweden.

- There is little evidence that UK organizations are adopting a strategic approach to flexible working. Few organizations make use of the full menu of flexibility and only a minority have explicit policies dealing with flexible working.

- There are widespread trends towards the widening of job roles for managers, technical/professional and clerical staff. This trend might at first thought be assumed to be quite universal in Europe. Yet national trends vary almost as much as in relation to contract and time flexibility.

- In summary, the research suggests that, with the exception of family-friendly flexibility, the UK is far from leading trends towards flexible working in Europe. The extent and diversity of flexible working practices is greater in a number of other countries, particularly the Netherlands.

## INTRODUCTION

Flexibility has been a major theme in employment and HRM policies for the last two decades. Employment flexibility is seen to be a key contributor to organizational as well as national competitiveness. True to its name, the term 'flexibility' is in itself flexible and can mean a number of things: cost-effective use of labour by matching working hours and overall labour costs to fluctuations in demand; non-standard ways of working; family-friendly employment practices to respond to changing social demands and to help recruit and retain the best employees; functional flexibility to allow organizations to adapt rapidly to new business opportunities and technological change. For policy makers, labour-market flexibility – the capacity of the economy to create new jobs and help people move from declining skills and sectors into expanding ones – adds another dimension.

Organizations now have much greater freedom than they have had for many decades to develop a targeted and custom-made approach to the way people are employed. They can draw on a broad menu of different practices to respond to the different drivers for flexibility in a focused and diversified manner. Such a response can have benefits beyond the immediate pressures by contributing to a broader change in culture and managerial practices in the organization. Yet these different drivers for flexibility do not always sit easily with each other. The question of whether it is possible to deliver on all flexibility fronts simultaneously – or whether indeed there are important trade-offs – has vexed British practitioners and academics since the beginning of these debates in the early 1980s.

It has been argued that the British labour market is the most flexible in Europe, since employers are less constrained by law in shaping the employment relationship in line with business requirements. This is particularly the case concerning the relative ease of hiring and firing people. The question is whether this 'numerical' flexibility to hire and fire is the major flexible advantage of the British economy or whether there has been a more fundamental change in the way people are employed towards a more varied and diversified manner of delivering flexibility for organizations. This chapter considers:

- different forms of flexibility: time and contract flexibility, family-friendly and employee-led flexibility, home-based working and teleworking;

- how far traditional employment patterns – with the majority of the workforce on permanent Monday-to-Friday type contracts – have been replaced, or at least significantly enriched, by a much greater diversity in how and when people are employed;

- where there is change, whether organizations are making use of the full menu of different working patterns available;

- functional flexibility and the narrowing and widening of job roles in the UK.

## TIME AND CONTRACT FLEXIBILITY

How 'standard' have 'non-standard' working practices become? Are people who work part-time, shifts, weekends, on temporary contracts or annualized hours still 'atypical', or is this term now truly a misnomer? The Cranet research provides a mixed picture. HR directors were asked whether there had been a change in the previous three years in the use of a range of flexible working practices. The most widespread growth has occurred in the employment of part-time and non-permanent workers: the large majority of organizations have reported increases consistently throughout the decade. Change has been less marked for other forms of time or contract flexibility such as shift working, weekend working or annualized hours (*see* Table 4.1). Time trends clearly suggest a cyclical dimension to developments – growth in all areas dipped during the recession of the early 1990s. However, throughout, in relation to all practices, the net effect has been an upward trend – the number of organizations moving away from a certain practice are always marginal and significantly outnumbered by those reporting growth.

| | UK 1990 | 1992 | 1995 | 1999 | EU 1999 |
|---|---|---|---|---|---|
| Part-time contracts | 41 | 39 | 50 | 54 | 47 |
| Temporary contracts | 59 | 39 | 60 | 49 | 41 |
| Fixed-term contracts | 26 | 29 | 47 | 40 | 49 |
| Weekend work | 24 | 17 | 27 | 29 | 8 |
| Shift work | 26 | 17 | 25 | 27 | 27 |
| Annualized hours | 7 | 11 | 15 | 16 | 25 |

**TABLE 4.1**

**Increase in time and contractual flexibility (in % of organizations)**

*"In the large majority of organizations flexible working applies to 10 per cent or less employees"*

Yet on a second measure of change the share of people on flexible working arrangements in the total workforce of each organization – the term 'non-standard' continues to be accurate in relation to most working patterns. With the exception of shift working and part-time work, which are more widespread, in the large majority of organizations flexible working applies to 10 per cent or less employees. Curiously, while the number of organizations using non-permanent contracts has increased and increased, the actual number of people on temporary and fixed-term contracts – who account for about 7 per cent of the UK workforce according to the Labour Force Survey (LFS) – has remained low. Labour economists are not fully sure of the reasons; one explanation is that companies draw on a small pool of people who are being rotated through a number of non-permanent appointments. Probably the statistics do not reflect the reality indicated by the employers in our survey and the huge growth in temporary employment agencies: people might simply be mistaken when they tell the LFS that they have a permanent contract.

A more detailed look at the UK pattern shows the importance of sectors of economic activity for an organization's choice of flexibility (*see* Tables 4.2 and 4.3). Shift working is clearly the most widespread time flexibility in manufacturing, and manufacturing firms also have the highest likelihood of having increased shift working. Part-time employment, on the other hand, continues to be rare in manufacturing and manufacturing firms are less likely to have seen growth in part-time employment. That said, four out of ten manufacturing firms reported growth in part-time employment in 1999, a not insignificant development. Part-time employment, in contrast, is the predominant form of flexibility in the public sector, and also has seen very widespread levels of growth. Unlike manufacturing, public-sector organizations also have a comparably high share of most other forms of flexibility; fixed-term employment is twice the national level for example, and annualized hours are also more widespread, as well as having grown proportionately in almost twice as many public-sector organizations than in the UK overall. However, shift working, also widespread in public services, has seen very little growth. From the survey, financial and business service firms are least likely to have embarked on time or contract flexibility; however, this might soon be a thing of the past as business-service firms have seen the highest growth rates in almost all areas of flexibility considered here.

| UK 1999 Manufacturing | Other industry | Business services | Other services | Public sector |
|---|---|---|---|---|
| Part-time contracts | 40 | 47 | 64 | 65 | 65 |
| Temporary contracts | 53 | 46 | 49 | 44 | 55 |
| Fixed-term contracts | 34 | 32 | 52 | 41 | 46 |
| Shift work | 37 | 24 | 30 | 21 | 13 |
| Weekend work | 27 | 27 | 41 | 31 | 27 |
| Annualized hours | 14 | 12 | 12 | 13 | 29 |

**TABLE 4.2**

**Increase in time and contractual flexibility by sector (in % of organizations)**

| | UK 1999 Manufac-turing | Other industry | Business services | Other services | Public sector | UK average | EU 1999 EU average |
|---|---|---|---|---|---|---|---|
| Shift work | 69 | 29 | 8 | 46 | 38 | 44 | 46 |
| Part-time contracts | 7 | 12 | 19 | 45 | 70 | 33 | 24 |
| Temporary contracts | 13 | 7 | 8 | 21 | 14 | 14 | 10 |
| Fixed-term contracts | 3 | 5 | 3 | 8 | 14 | 7 | 12 |
| Annualized hours | 11 | 10 | 3 | 4 | 13 | 9 | 16 |

**TABLE 4.3**

**Organizations where flexible workers account for more than 10 per cent of the workforce by sector (in %)**

## European comparisons

British trends in time and contract flexibility do not differ greatly from those in the EU as a whole (*see* Table 4.1). In relation to most practices, though, the average hides considerable diversity in national trends. Generally speaking, developments towards flexibility are more marked in the Nordic and middle European countries, while the southern countries, particularly Greece and Portugal, tend to lag behind. UK trends put it into the upper third of developments, but by no means in a leading position. This is taken by the Netherlands, where growth tends to be most pronounced across the different measures considered. The success of the Dutch economy to a significant extent is due to a flexibility pact between the social partners: employers, government and trade unions. Since the mid 1980s employees have agreed to a trade-off between wage increases and working time reductions; these have been implemented with a growing level of flexibility, leading to a wide menu of flexible working options aimed at responding both to employer and employee requirements for flexibility.

Part-time employment provides a good example for European diversity. Part-time employment in the EU is by far highest in the Netherlands, but the Scandinavian countries and the UK also have about a quarter of their workforces on part-time contracts, whereas levels in Greece, Italy, Spain and Portugal continue to be lower than 10 per cent. The Netherlands also has by far the highest proportion of organizations reporting further growth in part-time employment – almost a third higher than in the UK. Unlike the UK, though, in the other countries with high levels of part-time employment there is much less of a sector divide in relation to part-time work. Part-time working is spread much more widely through the whole economy.

Annualized hours provide another interesting example of national differences. In most countries growth has been rather moderate, ranging from about 3 per cent of organizations in Greece and Portugal to a fifth of organizations in Austria and the Netherlands. The one outstanding country here is France. Over four out of ten organizations reported an increase in annualized-hours contracts, and four out of ten organizations already have at least a tenth of their workforce on such contracts. While we have not investigated the reasons for this explosion in annualized hours contracts in detail, it is likely to be linked to employers' searches for flexibility and productivity gains against the background of the introduction of the statutory 35-hour week in France.

Finally, there is non-permanent employment. The UK is in the top third of EU countries in terms of reporting growth, but is at the bottom in terms of the absolute number of employees on such contracts. Non-permanent employment tends to be higher in countries with stronger employment legislation, but one country sticks out in particular: Spain. Here almost a third of the workforce is on non-permanent contracts, and while growth is not as high as in the Netherlands or the UK, it nevertheless occurred in the majority of organizations. Employment security was one of the quid pro quos of the Franco regime, and even though employment law has recently been amended to make it easier to dismiss people, companies are still wary of offering permanent contracts.

## FAMILY-FRIENDLY AND EMPLOYEE-LED FLEXIBILITY

The working practices reviewed so far in the main respond to drivers for more efficiency, even if they might also suit some employees. Part-time employment is the one least easily classified as efficiency driven as it clearly provides access to paid employment for many people whose domestic responsibilities preclude full-time work as an option. We included it in the efficiency or employer-led bundle of flexibility because, at least in the UK, there is considerable evidence that labour cost-related reasons are a major part of the motivation for part-time employment. We will now turn to employment flexibility, which is much more clearly employee driven:

- flexitime and flexible working hours

- job sharing

- home-based and teleworking.

## Flexitime

Flexitime is probably one of the earliest and quintessential introductions of employee-led flexibility and took off in the UK in the 1970s. Because of the rather bureaucratic nature of many flexitime schemes and, perhaps more importantly, the fact that the scale of flexibility and choice over working time is tipped firmly in the direction of the employee, the demise of flexitime schemes has frequently been predicted. This, however, is not confirmed by the Cranet Survey (*see* Table 4.4). Flexitime schemes are not spreading – less than a fifth of organizations have increased their use – but neither is there any evidence that they have gone out of fashion altogether. Once again, there are strong sector differences with public-sector organizations clearly most likely to have flexitime schemes and to have extended or changed them.

| | UK 1999 Manufac-turing | Other industry | Business services | Other services | Public sector | UK average | EU 1999 EU average |
|---|---|---|---|---|---|---|---|
| Organizations with flexitime schemes | 34 | 42 | 40 | 42 | 83 | 53 | 75 |
| Organizations having increased the use of flexitime schemes | 14 | 14 | 10 | 16 | 27 | 18 | 40 |

**TABLE 4.4**

**Flexitime schemes (% of organizations)**

Apart from Greece, the UK is the country with the lowest increase in flexitime in Europe. There is a wide range of developments across the EU. In the Netherlands over two thirds of organizations have widened their use of flexitime. Extensive growth has also taken place in Austria, Belgium, Germany and Sweden – in none of these countries from a low base. Flexitime was initially developed in Germany, where it is more widespread than in other EU countries. Administration of schemes is more likely to be automated there because it is common in Germany for non-manual employees as well as manual workers to clock in. Case studies from Germany and elsewhere suggest that flexitime schemes are not static and are moving on from their somewhat formal and rule-oriented origins. Flexitime schemes have been reinvented as an integral part of semi-autonomous work teams. Team members can negotiate between themselves who works when, as long as the operational demands of the team are fulfilled.

One reason perhaps for the wider spread of flexitime schemes in many other EU countries is the fact that working time in general is more strictly regulated – both by statute and, perhaps more importantly, by collective or workplace agreement – than in the UK. British employers can get significant flexibility in working time without setting up formal schemes. Indeed, the British Labour Force Survey suggests that unpaid overtime worked by full-time employees is the major form of flexibility in the UK. This is much less likely in countries such as Belgium, France, Germany, the Netherlands or Sweden. But while British employers have greater flexibility, they also have less of a curb on the long-hour culture, and hence less pressure to come up with solutions that allow a healthy work–life balance.

## Job sharing

One area in which the UK does lead is job sharing (*see* Table 4.5). Twice as many organizations in the UK as elsewhere in Europe have job-sharing schemes. Job sharing really took off in the 1990s as a means of attracting and retaining working mothers, who account for most – though not all – job sharers. During the 1990s there has been a marked trend in the number of women returning to work straight after their maternity leave. This has put life into many dormant job-share schemes that existed on paper but did not really have many takers. Job sharing has grown particularly in those sectors where there already is more experience with job sharing, above all public-sector organizations (*see* Table 4.6). In the public sector it is now much more common for managers faced with requests for job sharing to be able to turn to a colleague who already has experience with the ins and outs of setting up and managing job sharers. There is much less need for cajoling from the HR department and the 'I am all for job sharing in principle but this particular job cannot possibly be split' type of response has become less common (Hegewisch, 2000). Manufacturing employers, in contrast, are least likely to have job-sharing agreements. Nevertheless, the fact that at least four out of ten manufacturing employers now report they have job-sharing schemes is probably a good indicator of the manufacturing industry's concerns about recruiting and retaining more female employees.

| | UK 1990 | 1992 | 1995 | 1999 | EU 1999 |
|---|---|---|---|---|---|
| Organizations with job-share schemes | 33 | 35 | 57 | 63 | 45 |
| Organizations having increased the use of job sharing | n/a | n/a | 34 | 34 | 15 |

**TABLE 4.5**

**Job-share schemes (% of organizations)**

| | UK 1999 Manufacturing | Other industry | Business services | Other services | Public sector |
|---|---|---|---|---|---|
| Organizations with job-share schemes | 43 | 58 | 68 | 60 | 94 |
| Organizations having increased the use of job sharing | 22 | 36 | 37 | 36 | 50 |

**TABLE 4.6**

**Job-share schemes by sector (% of organizations)**

So why is job sharing so much less popular elsewhere in Europe? One reason is that UK employers are genuinely ahead in terms of equal opportunity policies, compared to most other countries in the EU, apart from the Nordic countries. The second reason is less positive. Job sharing is a way of opening part-time employment to those who are qualified and want to have a career job but are unable to work full-time. Thus job sharing is an acknowledgement that part-time jobs often are dead-end jobs, with little chance of genuine promotion and development. This problem of part-time jobs as second-class jobs is not unique to the UK, but it is much more pronounced here than elsewhere.

## Home-based and teleworking

The praises of home-based and teleworking and its potential for providing a better work–life balance for employees while generating efficiencies for the employer have been sung for many years. Yet growth remained distinctly sluggish for most of the last decade. However, the latest data suggest that finally such workplace flexibility might have moved out of the margins. Between 1995 and 1999 the share of organizations reporting an increase in home-based working almost doubled from 12 to 21 per cent (*see* Table 4.7); yet two thirds of organizations continue to report that home-based working is not used. Teleworking also increased, but with no more than one in ten organizations reporting growth and more than 80 per cent not using teleworking at all, it remains more marginal. Financial and business service firms clearly have made the biggest steps into the direction of workplace flexibility (*see* Table 4.8). Growth rates are almost double the national average, both in relation to home-based working and to teleworking. Manufacturing companies are least likely to allow people to work from home.

**TABLE 4.7**

**Increase in home-based and teleworking (in % of organizations)**

| | UK 1990 | 1992 | 1995 | 1999 | EU 1999 |
|---|---|---|---|---|---|
| Home-based working | 8 | 9 | 12 | 21 | 10 |
| Teleworking | n/a | n/a | 6 | 10 | 12 |

**TABLE 4.8**

**Increase in home-based and teleworking by sector (in % of organizations)**

| | UK 1999 Manufacturing | Other industry | Business services | Other services | Public sector | UK average | EU 1999 EU average |
|---|---|---|---|---|---|---|---|
| Home-based working | 12 | 23 | 39 | 26 | 21 | 21 | 10 |
| Teleworking | 6 | 10 | 23 | 11 | 6 | 10 | 12 |

The Cranet Survey does not include a specific definition of home-based working or teleworking: responses therefore can include people who work exclusively from home or people who occasionally work from home, or indeed, who hardly work from home at all but are mostly out of the office because they are visiting clients, for example. This comparative vagueness is a common issue in research in this field; neither the Labour Force Survey nor the 1998 Workplace Employee Relations Survey include a detailed definition. What is clear from the latter survey, however, is that in the large majority of workplaces home-based working is only used for part of the week – it is rare to have employees exclusively working from home. In this sense home-based working is perhaps a misnomer: 'locational' flexibility or 'out-of-office' working is perhaps a more accurate description of home-based and teleworking.

In many ways the managerial issues are the same whether people are out of the office because they work from home or because they are on the road or with clients. Those organizations making use of home-based working certainly find that it raises new management issues. More explicit communication strategies and a review of performance management tools are the obvious ones. There is evidence that such working can be problematic for (isolated) individuals, too, and there are also difficulties in dealing with the perceptions of 'second-class citizenship' amongst those employees not able to work from home – often the ones who provide the administrative backbone of organizations.

Compared to the EU overall, British organizations seem to be more adventurous in terms of introducing home-based working. Yet UK trends significantly lag behind those in some other EU member states. Over a third of Danish and Swedish employers increased home-based working, and over six out of ten Swedish employers increased teleworking; developments in Denmark and the Netherlands are not as exceptional but are still over double the UK levels.

## Strategic decisions or *ad hoc* responses?

In the UK and elsewhere there has been some discussion about the nature of change in employment patterns. Employers may be systematically evaluating and implementing the opportunities accorded by more varied working patterns or may be developing *ad hoc* responses to circumstances. In a quantitative survey such as Cranet it is not easy to provide reliable tests of strategic intent for flexibility. Yet several indicators suggest that on the whole the undoubted growth in flexible working patterns is not the result of strategic corporate decisions. First, with the exception of the public sector, the large majority of organizations do not have written flexible working policies (*see* Table 4.9); indeed almost four out of ten organizations profess to have no policies at all in this area. The absence of written policies is, of course, not yet evidence of the absence of strategic intent; yet it does suggest a limit to the proactive use of flexibility, whether in relation to productivity or to culture change. Second, the majority of organizations focus their move towards flexibility on one or two working patterns. The share of organizations increasing at least three forms of flexibility, out of the nine forms considered in the survey, is less than 10 per cent of the sample (the most popular combination is part-time work, shift working and non-permanent employment). Yet a strategic approach to flexibility would suggest the exploration of the full menu of options, not falling back on one or two ways of responding to needs for flexibility. Incidentally, the organizations with a more diversified increase in flexible working are not more likely to have flexible working policies than the others.

**TABLE 4.9**

**Organizations with written flexible-working policies by sector (in %)**

| UK 1999 Manufacturing | Other industry | Business services | Other services | Public sector | UK average | EU 1999 EU average |
|---|---|---|---|---|---|---|
| 32 | 27 | 32 | 28 | 61 | 38 | 46 |

Instead of being the result of strategic decisions, the growth in employment flexibility is more likely to be the result of allowing line departments greater freedom over employment decisions. In principle such an approach has the benefit of allowing room for experimentation and allowing managers to respond more closely to local labour-market pressures. However, the data suggest that rather than experiment and try something new, line managers are perhaps rather more likely to fall back on what has been tried and tested already. Thus innovation does not necessarily flow from decentralization (Mayne *et al*, 2000).

## FUNCTIONAL FLEXIBILITY

The time when British industry was seen as synonymous with rigid job demarcations is long gone. However, the challenge of keeping work organization and skills flexible enough to deal with the rapidly changing business environment if anything is bigger now than when demarcations were a major employee-relations issue. The Cranet data certainly show that few organizations have left job roles alone during the 1990s; on the whole they have increased the scope of jobs (*see* Table 4.10). Managerial jobs have seen most change recently, but clerical and technical/ professional job roles are not far behind. Manual jobs have been the subject of less change compared to other employee groups; one reason is that manual workers were probably the first target of job restructuring, and the shift away from traditional ways of working has been implemented for longer. The second reason is more profane: manual workers are more likely to be a small minority of workers in organizations, and hence less essential to overall reorganization. Where they make up a substantial number of the workforce, trends towards flexibility are little different from the other groups.

| | UK 1992 | 1995 | 1999 | EU 1999 |
|---|---|---|---|---|
| Management: | | | | |
| jobs widened | 45 | 58 | 53 | 51 |
| jobs narrowed | 25 | 19 | 26 | 23 |
| Professional/technical: | | | | |
| jobs widened | 37 | 48 | 46 | 50 |
| jobs narrowed | 20 | 17 | 24 | 28 |
| Clerical: | | | | |
| jobs widened | 41 | 51 | 51 | 47 |
| jobs narrowed | 12 | 11 | 14 | 19 |
| Manual: | | | | |
| jobs widened | 38 | 43 | 39 | 38 |
| jobs narrowed | 9 | 7 | 9 | 14 |

**TABLE 4.10**

**Organizations reporting widening or narrowing job roles for major staff categories during the previous three years (in %)**

Personnel directors were asked whether job roles had widened/become more flexible or had narrowed/become more specific. The widening of job roles can include a number practices, from formal job rotation or job-enrichment policies to less formal changes where jobs have grown more or less by default. The number of organizations saying that they use job rotation as part of their employee development is – at 30 per cent – considerably lower than the number reporting a widening of job roles overall, suggesting that at least some of the change is less structured and developmental.

However, change does not necessarily imply that jobs have been widened. A substantial number of organizations – a quarter in the case of managers and professional and technical staff – have introduced less rather than more flexibility and have narrowed down job roles. It is not totally clear why. More active performance management might be one reason: there has been a more systematic review of who does what as a way of pinning down performance criteria, and this focus on the way work is done might also lead to limitations on the scope of jobs.

These trends are replicated across all sectors of the economy with only minor differences in 1999 (*see* Table 4.11). This was quite different at the beginning of the 1990s when developments in manufacturing by far outstripped those in the public sector, business services and banking. But

*"A substantial number of organizations have introduced less rather than more flexibility and have narrowed down job roles"*

while differences have diminished in relation to the widening of job roles, they have not in relation to the narrowing of job roles: in each year of the Cranet Survey public-sector employers have been more likely than other employers to have made job roles more specific, for all employee groups. Productivity and work organization in public-sector organizations have been under intense scrutiny for much of the 1990s, in response to initiatives such as market testing, tendering and outsourcing of non-manual services. The redefinition of job roles might be one outcome. Alternatively, and more provocatively, it might be a symptom of a continued greater rule orientation in parts of the public sector.

**TABLE 4.11**

**Organizations reporting widening or narrowing job roles for major staff categories by sector (in %)**

| | UK 1999 Manufacturing | Other industry | Business services | Other services | Public sector |
|---|---|---|---|---|---|
| **Management:** | | | | | |
| jobs widened | 55 | 52 | 48 | 55 | 50 |
| jobs narrowed | 23 | 11 | 27 | 25 | 34 |
| **Professional/technical:** | | | | | |
| jobs widened | 51 | 55 | 45 | 42 | 42 |
| jobs narrowed | 21 | 14 | 26 | 21 | 30 |
| **Clerical:** | | | | | |
| jobs widened | 56 | 48 | 54 | 49 | 45 |
| jobs narrowed | 10 | 5 | 15 | 16 | 16 |
| **Manual:** | | | | | |
| jobs widened | 55 | 36 | 18 | 41 | 34 |
| jobs narrowed | 9 | 4 | 0 | 11 | 11 |

## No universal trend towards functional flexibility

The trend away from tight job descriptions might at first be assumed to be reasonably universal across Europe. Certainly, global competition does not stop at borders. However, national trends in functional flexibility vary almost as much as in relation to time and contractual flexibility. This applies even in relation to managers, who are least likely to be covered by collective bargaining or statute in relation to their job roles. French organizations, for example, are only half as likely as UK ones to have made managerial jobs more flexible and, more interestingly perhaps, French organizations introducing more detailed job control of managers outnumber those making jobs more flexible. This is also the case in Finland and Greece. French managers, or *cadres*, are subject to greater regulation than in most EU countries, with greater external comparability and rules of promotion and reward. International studies show French companies to be more hierarchical, with more layers of management, than British, German or Swedish firms. Thus the trends are not due to a more flexible starting point. Sweden, on the other hand, sticks out by being the country with the lowest likelihood of tightened job roles, across all staff categories. The Netherlands is the country that consistently has the strongest trend towards greater job flexibility. These differences perhaps are a testament to the continued cultural diversity across Europe. The definition of job roles are closely linked to issues of trust, hierarchy and delegation; studies of cultural differences in attitudes at work, and particularly in managerial roles, show that Europe is one of the most diverse regions in the world (Hofstede, 1991).

## Training and job flexibility

How far do organizations put training behind the increase in responsibilities for their employees? The 1998 British Workplace Employee Relations Survey asked managers specifically whether employees were trained to be multi-skilled, in the sense of being able to perform a job other than their own; they found that in less than a quarter of organizations a clear majority of employees were trained to be functionally flexible, and in most of the remaining organizations there was no such training or only for a small minority of workers (Cully *et al*, 1999). But perhaps such a definition is rather tight and will not capture many of the changes where employees have been given increased responsibility, though within the broad remit of their job or profession. The Cranet research did not directly investigate whether employers support bigger jobs with more training. However, in the UK, clerical and manual workers on average receive significantly more training in organizations that have broadened their job roles; professional, technical and managerial staff do not. This has to be set in context: average training levels are in any case twice as high for managers and professionals than for the other groups (*see* Chapter 5). In the EU overall there is also no evidence of a positive link between job role flexibility and training levels, but once again for clerical and manual workers training levels are on average higher than in the UK.

The issue of training and skill development has also been a key policy issue in relation to contractual flexibility. Studies by the Confederation of British Industry (CBI), and by the Organization for Economic Co-operation and Development (OECD) internationally, point to a decline in the overall skill pool because of the increase in 'non-standard' workers: employers have less incentive to train if employees stay only for relatively short periods. This is certainly borne out by research on temporary and non-permanent workers. While these workers are generally just as likely to be content in their jobs, access to training and development is the area where they feel disadvantaged compared to permanent workers. However, at the level of the firm, both the Cranet Survey and the 1998 Workplace Employee Relations Survey if anything find a positive association between training levels and the level of non-permanent staff, perhaps because it tends to be in skilled and professional jobs that non-permanent staff are employed. This seems to be a UK-specific characteristic. In countries such as France, Spain or Sweden – all with a high level of non-permanent employment – companies employing a high proportion of non-permanent staff do less well on training.

## Job flexibility v. contractual flexibility?

There has been some discussion, at least among labour market policy makers, of the potential trade-off between an HR strategy mainly based on skills-based flexibility against one mainly based on labour cost and numerical flexibility. The European Commission, for example, refers to these respectively as the 'high' and 'low' roads to competitiveness and firmly favours the former: an approach based on functional flexibility, training, employee involvement and quality. At the macro-economic level, comparing different EU countries, there is some evidence in support of such a polarity in approaches. But at the micro level, comparing different organizations, there is less evidence for such a dualism. Organizations that have implemented a significant change towards more flexible jobs are less likely to have a high level of non-permanent employees, but the differences are marginal and it is more likely that such links are accidental – not just in the statistical sense, but also as an outcome of decentralized HR decision making. However, organizations who have a comparatively high level of non-permanent staff are less likely – both in Europe and the UK – to rank themselves as top performers in relation to service quality or productivity.

*"Organizations are more willing to experiment with new ways of organizing work"*

## CONCLUSION

During the last ten years the landscape of work has seen considerable changes. Organizations are more willing to experiment with new ways of organizing work, and the share of people who are permanently employed and work regular full-time weekday hours has declined. Yet rather than trying out a range of work options, organizations seem to turn to the new standard 'non-standard': part-time work and non-permanent employment. More innovative arrangements, be they annualized hours, job sharing, teleworking or home-based working, continue to be quite marginal in the overall picture in the UK.

Our research also suggests that the UK is far from leading the trends towards flexible working in Europe. The extent and diversity of flexible working practices is greater in a number of countries, particularly in the Netherlands. The higher level of regulation of working time and work organization in most other EU countries is forcing these European employers to take a more proactive approach to flexibility. UK organizations, however, clearly lead the field when it comes to developing family-friendly policies, and particular, job sharing.

## REFERENCES

Cully, M., Woodland, S., O'Reilly, A. & Dix, A. (1999) *Britain at Work: As depicted by the 1998 Workplace Employee Relations Survey*. London: Routledge.

Hegewisch, A. (2000) *Flexible Working Patterns in Local Government*. London: Employers Association for Local Government.

Hofstede, G. (1991) *Cultures and Organizations: Software of the mind*. London: McGraw Hill.

Mayne, L., Tregaskis, O. & Brewster, C. (2000) 'A comparative analysis of the link between flexibility and HRM strategy' in C.J. Brewster, W. Mayrhofer & M. Morley (eds) *New Challenges for European Human Resource Management*. London: Macmillan.

McShane, D. and Brewster, C. (2000) *Making Flexibility Work*. London: Fabian Society (pamphlet 595).

# Employee development

## EXECUTIVE SUMMARY

Employee development is a crucial element of HRM and, in the new knowledge economy, is being given ever higher prominence by organizations in Europe.

The key points are:

- In 1999 the budget allocated by organizations to employee development was (on average and across sectors) 3 per cent of annual salaries; the business services sector invested significantly more.

- This level of budgeting for employee development compared well with continental Europe, with the exception of the building and transport sectors where the UK lagged behind the majority of its EU competitors.

- UK organizations are spreading their training effort to a growing proportion of the workforce. However, managers and professionals are far more likely to receive training and development than lower-levels employees.

- The priorities for management training in the UK include: the management of people, the management of technology and the management of change. These areas have dominated the training agenda over the last decade and are set, despite changes in emphasis, to remain critical in the future.

- UK organizations closely monitor the effectiveness of training. Doing so provides performance indicators that are helpful both in terms of improving the quality of training and in terms of quantifying the contribution of HR to business performance.

- A significant proportion of HR managers claims to monitor training effectiveness on the basis of behavioural changes, an area which is increasingly attracting interest.

- In terms of managerial development, UK practitioners have a bias for career planning and are increasingly likely to use assessment centres. Practices in other EU countries vary widely.

- The 1999 Cranet Survey indicates a significant increase in the use of appraisals, particularly for lower categories of staff. Furthermore, the survey reveals that in the UK appraisals are mostly seen as an opportunity for mapping out personal development. In other EU nations the emphasis is different and appraisals are used more often than in the UK to determine performance-related pay.

- Overall, employee development is seen as part of wider HR strategic objectives and not just as a set of intermittent and unrelated interventions.

## INTRODUCTION

Training and development has received considerable attention over the past decade, both in the UK and other European countries. Governments in particular have been keen to investigate ways in which to improve current training provisions, so as to develop a pool of workers and managers who can better cope with the challenges of the information age. Indeed, the rate of change, new technologies and the increased need for creative skills require increasing attention to employee development.

The competitive advantages to be achieved through using best practice in training are significant. Smart companies use training to support their strategic and business objectives. Hence training and development can be an essential element in bringing about organizational change. Multinational enterprises are increasingly setting up their own corporate universities, a pattern that started in the US (e.g. Kellogg's University, or those of McDonald's or General Motors) and becoming more common in Europe (e.g. Thomson University, France; Lufthansa University, Germany). Such centres for learning not only facilitate the acquisition of new skills, they are also the carriers and shapers of organizational culture, providing space and facilities for people from various departments, subsidiaries, or even countries to come together. These serve a unique purpose beyond learning – namely, creating and reinforcing a sense of organizational identity and common vision. These examples are indications that training should not be seen as an *ad hoc* process; rather, it is an essential component of organizational life and employee development.

The development of employees in the workplace is essential for all categories of staff and can play a significant role in any change or integration process (e.g. mergers and take-overs and the ensuing integration of a diverse workforce). Increasingly, smaller organizations, which may not have the facilities and budgets to match best practice, none the less recognize the value of training and development. They do this not only to improve skills but also to enable them to implement wider strategic objectives.

This chapter covers questions such as:

- how much (expenditure and budgeting)
- who (recipients of training)
- what (key areas for training)
- how (delivery mechanisms)
- how well (monitoring the effectiveness of training)
- so what (management development, appraisal).

## TRAINING EXPENDITURE

Throughout the last decade British organizations invested, on average, 2.8 per cent of annual salary and wage bills on training. In 1999 there was a marginal increase over previous years, reflecting the strength of the economy and a greater willingness to invest in training and development (*see* Table 5.1)

| | UK 1990 | 1992 | 1995 | 1999 | EU 1999 |
|---|---|---|---|---|---|
| % of annual salaries spent on training | 2.7 | 2.7 | 2.6 | 3.0 | 3.2 |

**TABLE 5.1**

**Median spending levels on training and development (as % of annual wages and salary bill)**

The survey results are, however, more revealing when broken down into industry sectors and set in the light of European comparisons. This shows that across the EU organizations operating in business services have invested significantly more than organizations in other sectors (*see* Table 5.2). In the UK the proportion of annual salaries spent on training in business services was 4.4 per cent (above the same sectorial EU average: 4.1 per cent). In France business services invested as much as 5.3 per cent. These findings for 1999 reflect two unusual factors: first, the investments necessary to cope with the introduction of the Euro and second, the necessity to deal safely with the IT implications of the transition to the year 2000. HR practitioners in the financial sector thus made the biggest effort in terms of training budgets.

At the other end of the scale, the public sector in the UK only invested 2.3 per cent of annual salaries in training and development in 1999. This is somewhat low compared to other sectors in the UK but in line with the public-sector average in the EU (2.2 per cent). In any case, it should rise as the Chancellor announced extra funding for the public sector in his 2000 budget. In contrast to the UK, Belgium stands out for record high investments in the public sector (5 per cent), reflecting a tradition of state support. Investments were also quite high in the Finnish and Swedish public sector (3.6 per cent and 3.4 per cent respectively) but, contrary to Belgium, remained below their national expenditure average (Zander, 1999).

**TABLE 5.2**

**Median spending levels on training and development, by sector (as % of annual wages and salary bill)**

|  | Manufacturing | Other industry | Business services | Other services | Public sector |
|---|---|---|---|---|---|
| UK 1999 | 3.0 | 2.4 | 4.4 | 3.0 | 2.3 |
| EU 1999 | 3.0 | 3.9 | 4.1 | 3.4 | 2.2 |

In the manufacturing industry the UK was on the same footing as its European competitors (3 per cent in 1999). Investments in the manufacturing sector also reflect the UK national average. These findings are particularly good news for this sector of industry, suggesting that the UK has caught up with EU competitors and is no longer lagging behind, as had been reported by Lane (1989), Glover & Hughes (1996) and Tregaskis (1997). Still, French organizations in the manufacturing sector spent more than their European counterparts with investments reaching 4.9 per cent in 1999. Legislation in France encourages organizations across all industry sectors to invest a high proportion of their payroll in training and development – and to have detailed accounting procedures. This legislative framework directly impacts on the level of training provision, especially in the manufacturing sector.

*"Over the last decade, organizations in the UK have gradually increased investments dedicated to training and development"*

The largest discrepancy between the UK and EU figures lies in other industries, including building and transport. Here the UK under-invests significantly (2.4 per cent) compared to the EU average (3.9 per cent).

Summing up, in terms of training budgets the UK compares well with European competitors, albeit marginally below EU average. None the less, the UK does stand out with high levels of investments in the traditionally strong area of business services. The under-funded sectors of industry remain building and transport. Overall, over the last decade, organizations in the UK have gradually increased the proportional levels of investments dedicated to training and development.

## RECIPIENTS OF TRAINING

Who are the recipients of such investments in training and development? In the UK quite a large proportion of employees (54 per cent) took part in some internal or external training activity in 1999. This figure is largely above the EU average (43 per cent). In fact, of all our European competitors, only Finland and Sweden did better in spreading the training effort to as many people as possible (respectively 61 per cent and 65 per cent of their workforces). However, 54 per cent for the UK is an encouraging result and is worth emphasizing as it reflects the best practice of UK organizations when it comes to distributing training to a wide proportion of employees. In addition, and perhaps critically, compared to EU competitors the UK presents lower cash investment correlated with greater amounts of training. Is it the case that the UK is under-investing and trying to get its training on the cheap? Or is it the case that training spending is used more wisely and cost-effectively in the UK? An explanation would require more research. At this stage, it is only possible to point out that the large proportion of employees taking part in training activities in the UK appears to be unrelated to a bias towards on-the-job versus off-the-job training. In fact, a number of European competitors are dramatically increasing the proportion of on-the-job training; in the UK the increase is less sharp.

What the survey does show is that there are differences in the provision of training to different categories of staff. Indeed, on average in 1999, UK managers and professionals were likely to receive more than twice as many days' training as clerical and manual employees (*see* Table 5.3). A clear split appears between managerial/professional on the one hand and clerical/manual on the other. There has been little variation in this split between the two sets of categories over the last decade.

| | UK 1992 | 1995 | 1999 | EU 1999 |
|---|---|---|---|---|
| Management | 5 | 4 | 5 | 6 |
| Professional | 5 | 4 | 5 | 6 |
| Clerical | 3 | 2 | 2 | 4 |
| Manual | 2 | 2 | 2 | 4 |

**TABLE 5.3**

**Median number of training days per category of employee**

Unlike for training expenditure, hardly any variance exists between industry sectors in terms of the number of training days received per staff category. Clerical and manual employees consistently receive less training than management and professional staff across industry sectors.

This split is not as clear-cut in other EU countries. For instance, in the sector of financial and business services, in Spain and Denmark clerical workers received exactly the same number of training days as managers. In a different sector of industry, that of building and transport, in Sweden clerical workers even received more training than their managers. It appears that in UK organizations there is a hierarchy that favours managers and professionals. Such a hierarchy of training at the top rather than at the bottom is worth challenging. Is it appropriate in a service economy? Arguably, customer-focused business strategies can only be implemented if front-line employees, who are critical to service levels, receive an equal share of training as other categories of staff.

Hence in the UK not all categories of staff benefit equally from training. Variations are less evident in other countries. Examples demonstrate that a hierarchy favouring managers and professionals as opposed to clerical and manual workers is not the norm everywhere and that there is room for HR managers in the UK to examine critically who benefits most from investments in training across all categories of staff.

## KEY AREAS OF TRAINING

The key training areas identified by the senior HR specialists responding to the Cranet Survey have remained constant throughout the last decade. The top four are the management of people (supervising), information technology, the management of change and customer service skills. These topics receive equally high rankings from HR practitioners in other European countries, thus pointing to a convergence of interests at the European level.

Table 5.4 presents the results for the UK and the marginal variance between 1995 and 1999. The variance is relatively minimal; the largest differential between 1995 and 1999 is an 11 per cent drop in the preference for training in change management. The results therefore show remarkable stability.

| | UK 1995 | 1999 | EU 1999 |
|---|---|---|---|
| People management and supervision | 80 | 81 | 61 |
| Computers and new technology | 59 | 64 | 52 |
| Management of change | 65 | 54 | 41 |
| Customer-service skills | 56 | 50 | 50 |
| Quality management | 47 | 36 | 38 |
| Health, safety and work environment | 34 | 33 | 20 |
| Strategy formulation | 37 | 31 | 25 |
| Marketing and sales | 35 | 27 | 28 |
| Business administration | 15 | 11 | 16 |

**TABLE 5.4**

**Areas of training 'very important' to organizations over the next three years (in % of organizations)**

Topical issues do change but remain within the same paradigm. Thus under the umbrella of the management of people, an organization seeking to expand across borders may seek particular managerial training on topics such as cross-cultural management, whereas prior to internationalization, managerial training may have focused on managing people within one's domestic environment. Nevertheless, the core objective of training – managing people – remains the same but the focus has changed in line with the strategic direction of the organization.

Under the umbrella of technology, training is similarly updated regularly to match the short life cycle of IT products. Hence training needs do evolve over time, but in the UK – and beyond – they do so within the strategic themes of people, technology, change and customer service.

However, care needs to be taken when interpreting these figures. Sectoral breakdowns give a more representative picture (*see* Table 5.5). The findings show, for instance, that health and safety training is taken much more seriously in the building and transport industry (52 per cent of the UK respondents indicated it was very important) than in business services, where health and safety issues were only considered by 8 per cent of UK HR practitioners to be very important. Such results clearly reflect sectoral priorities. Safety is much more important for employees working on a building site or in transportation than for office-bound employees. Another example of sectoral bias is the area of customer-service skills. These skills are considered to be very important by 67 per cent of HR practitioners in the service sector; in other industry sectors (manufacturing, building, transport, other industry and public sector) service skills are seen as less important, with scores ranging from 41 per cent to 46 per cent. Another point raised by the Cranet Survey is the increasing importance of information technology and the need to train employees in using new technology. Over the coming years IT will be a high priority in the public sector and in business services.

**TABLE 5.5**

**Areas of training 'very important' to organizations over the next three years by sector (in % of organizations) (1999)**

| | UK 1999 Manufacturing | Other industry | Business services | Other services | Public sector |
|---|---|---|---|---|---|
| People management and supervision | 80 | 74 | 79 | 82 | 84 |
| Computers and new technology | 55 | 61 | 66 | 63 | 73 |
| Management of change | 52 | 53 | 57 | 48 | 62 |
| Customer-service skills | 41 | 44 | 67 | 67 | 46 |
| Quality management | 35 | 26 | 29 | 28 | 53 |
| Health, safety and work environment | 39 | 53 | 8 | 31 | 36 |
| Strategy formulation | 32 | 26 | 28 | 31 | 33 |
| Marketing and sales | 34 | 30 | 40 | 32 | 7 |
| Business administration | 10 | 9 | 7 | 15 | 11 |

*"The best business strategy will fail if an organization does not have the right workforce"*

Despite variations in terms of training priorities reflecting the context and extant strategic priorities of a particular sector, the areas of training identified as the management of people, the management of technology and the management of change remain stable across sectors. The most critical area of training for the UK is by far the management of people. The best business strategy and financial plan will fail if an organization does not have the right workforce, able to do the right things in the right ways.

## Identification of training needs

The majority of HR practitioners in the UK have been constantly aware, throughout the decade, of the requirement to conduct a training needs analysis (TNA). Table 5.6 illustrates this stability. While most HR practitioners do conduct a TNA, there has been no progress over time. Yet best practice shows that a TNA is essential.

| | UK 1990 | 1992 | 1995 | 1999 | EU 1999 |
|---|---|---|---|---|---|
| Yes | 82 | 82 | 80 | 83 | 77 |
| No | 16 | 19 | 19 | 16 | 22 |
| Don't know | 1 | – | 1 | 2 | 1 |

TABLE 5.6

Systematic analysis of employee training needs (in % of organizations)

The responses from other EU countries similarly indicate that HR managers do systematically analyze training needs (the EU average is 77 per cent). Denmark stands out with a relatively lower score: less than six of every ten of their managers claim to analyze training needs (1999 survey).

The UK respondents who indicated that they did systematically analyze training needs, were asked which method they would normally use. Table 5.7 highlights the importance of regular performance appraisals as a means to identify formally training needs. Indeed, the use of performance appraisals has, over the last decade, consistently been the UK's favourite method of identifying training needs. The UK also stands out significantly amongst all other EU nations as making the most use of this method. This may reflect a cultural tradition that encourages a relatively informal communication style between employees and managers. Performance appraisals are a systematic attempt to assess past performance as much as to discuss career developments for individuals. They require a culture where employees and managers are comfortable discussing such issues in a more or less informal way (Lawrence & Edwards, 2000).

| | UK 1992 | 1995 | 1999 | EU 1999 |
|---|---|---|---|---|
| Performance appraisal | 52 | 54 | 59 | 39 |
| Analysis of projected business/service plans | 30 | 29 | 34 | 28 |
| Line-management requests | 31 | 23 | 30 | 40 |
| Training audits | 20 | 17 | 20 | 35 |
| Employee requests | 14 | 11 | 16 | 19 |

TABLE 5.7

Methods used to analyze training needs (in % of organizations)

UK managers are also keen to use projected business plans to inform their training programmes, reflecting an endeavour to link business strategy to HR strategy. In comparison to the UK, Scandinavian countries such as Sweden, Denmark, and Finland tend to make less use of such projected business plans. Given the track record for high standards of HR in these countries, the subject of linking business and HR plans most certainly deserves an in-depth debate by HR practitioners in the EU and ought to be the focus for future research.

A particularly interesting finding is the use of line-management requests as a means of identifying training needs. In France and some other Mediterranean nations such as Spain and Greece this is quite common, whereas the UK and other northern nations resort to this less. Seven out of ten organizations in France use line-management requests to identify training needs, perhaps reflecting the hierarchical managerial structure in that country. This confirms the established principle of the single chain of command (emphasis on line management) that reigns in French organizations (Pettinger, 1994; Barsoux and Lawrence, 1997).

Overall, UK organizations may be leading the best practice in terms of using performance appraisals to identify training needs to a much greater extent than other EU nations. However, only one in five organizations in the UK actually carry out training audits, whereas many more organizations do so in the EU. UK HR professionals are good at performance appraisals and projected business plans, but what about thorough training audits?

## TRAINING DELIVERY

Having established the areas of training that are of crucial importance to HR practitioners in the UK, it is helpful to explore how these topics are delivered. Learning can take place through various means, and companies are increasingly looking at fostering alternative ways of learning. Noticeably, they are taking a keen interest in training being delivered through computer-based packages. Indeed, in the last survey, 51 per cent of UK respondents predict an increase in the use of such technology to deliver training (*see* Table 5.8). A senior British HR manager invited to comment on the findings points out:

> We no longer simply have a computer room. Now, the training packages can be downloaded from the intranet. Personally, I find it a fun thing to do. However, the impact of providing such tools is hard to evaluate. Currently we provide the investment, assuming that it is a good thing in itself, in line with learning-organization ideas. In the future there might be more emphasis on the pay-back and evaluation.

| | UK 1999 Increased | Decreased | EU 1999 Increased | Decreased |
|---|---|---|---|---|
| Computer-based packages | 51 | 2 | 38 | 1 |
| Coaching/mentoring | 52 | 1 | 34 | 2 |
| Internal training staff | 52 | 10 | 44 | 7 |
| On-the-job training | 48 | 1 | 43 | 3 |
| External training providers | 47 | 11 | 49 | 7 |
| Line managers | 41 | 3 | 28 | 4 |

**TABLE 5.8**

**Changes in the means of delivering training over the last three years (in % of organizations)**

On the whole, however, the figures reveal an increase in all categories of delivery. This reflects the fact that HR practitioners have enlarged their options and are matching the delivery of training programmes to their various needs. Towards the end of the decade, in the UK, the trend was for training to take place through coaching and mentoring, as well as under the guidance of internal training staff. The UK organizations are therefore keen to use and pass on the knowledge acquired from within to parts of the same organization that could also benefit from it.

In the EU the same delivery routes are on an increase, but the greatest increase is in the use of external training providers. In the South in particular (i.e. France, Spain and Portugal), HR practitioners were not as keen as in the UK to implement coaching and mentoring. Hence knowledge was sought from outside the organization. In Ireland and Austria, organizations increased their use of external training providers by 60 per cent and above.

## MONITORING OF TRAINING EFFECTIVENESS

Following the identification of training needs and having delivered appropriate training programmes, the question is raised of measuring the value of such programmes. HR managers are increasingly challenged to demonstrate their contribution to overall business performance. Measuring the effectiveness of training is a relatively easy way of providing performance indicators, which are also essential to improve quality. Not surprisingly, the vast majority of organizations claim to measure training effectiveness.

In the EU the managers most assiduously claiming to monitor training effectiveness are the French and the Italians, closely followed by the British. The 1999 Cranet Survey reveals that 83 per cent of British organizations monitor the effectiveness of their training. Overall however, only 67 per cent of EU organizations claim to monitor the effectiveness of training. UK organizations are therefore comparing well.

The survey also reveals at what point these managers evaluate training (*see* Table 5.9). In the majority of cases training effectiveness is evaluated immediately after training. However, evaluation some months after training is becoming increasingly common. Indeed, best practice does recommend that training be evaluated some months after delivery. In that way organizations are able to assess the long-term impact of training. In the UK 42 per cent of HR managers claim sometimes to evaluate training some months after.

**TABLE 5.9**

**How often formal evaluation is used (in % of organizations)**

| | Immediately after training | | Some months after training | |
|---|---|---|---|---|
| | UK 1999 | EU 1999 | UK 1999 | EU 1999 |
| Always | 68 | 59 | 18 | 14 |
| Often | 24 | 28 | 33 | 30 |
| Sometimes | 7 | 10 | 42 | 44 |
| Never | 1 | 3 | 7 | 11 |

The 1999 survey also sought to understand the ways in which HR practitioners assess training. The results reveal that the most common way of measuring training effectiveness is to ask the recipients to rate their level of satisfaction of the training event. Hence, in 94 per cent of cases, training is evaluated on the basis of the 'reaction' of participants (*see* Table 5.10).

**TABLE 5.10**

**Systematic evaluation of training (in % of organizations)**

| | UK 1999 | EU 1999 |
|---|---|---|
| Reaction/evaluation (e.g. satisfaction expressed by employees) | 94 | 85 |
| Learning (usually assessed by a test) | 41 | 36 |
| Behaviour (changes in job performance) | 81 | 67 |
| Results (changes in organizational performance) | 67 | 58 |

Since the 'reaction' of participants is so systematically evaluated, best-practice organizations have to look for other meaningful measures to evaluate the impact of training. A number of organizations do so by assessing learning through a test. This is to be commended as it is fairly straightforward and often focuses the attention of the participants and that of the trainers on issues that are of crucial importance in the training programme. This may be especially important in health and safety training.

Increasingly, organizations claim to measure changes in job performance as a measure of whether training has actually been effective. This is particularly relevant for operative, manual and clerical workers, whose tasks may be drastically improved by the implementation of a new process. It is also relevant for other levels, such as professionals and managers, whose behavioural changes can be assessed, particularly through the use of performance appraisals.

A surprising finding is that 67 per cent of British managers claim to measure systematically the impact of training on 'results'. A UK HR director comments: 'Systematically? No, No! I wonder myself under what circumstances would it be possible to truthfully answer "yes" to the question of measuring the impact on results. Maybe there is a danger that respondents may have considered "ought to be" values.' Clearly, whether these results truly reflect HR activities or whether they reflect their wishful thinking, one may safely conclude that British HR managers are seeking to measure more and more precisely their contribution to overall business performance and want to be seen as doing so.

*"Increasingly, organizations claim to measure changes in job performance as a measure of whether training has actually been effective"*

Another British manager who took part in the panel commenting on these results asked very pragmatically: 'Do people have the time? Are they able to take time to develop themselves? Again and again, they simply cannot find the time. We have currently adopted as our best proxy measure the fact that "managers are so ... busy, if they turn up, they must value the training"!'

According to the survey findings, HR managers in other EU countries also seem quite keen to measure the effectiveness of training on behaviour and results. For instance, nine out of ten Italian practitioners claim to measure changes in behaviour – by all standards an overwhelming score. Challenging this view, only one in ten Dutch managers claims to measure changes in behaviour.

## MANAGEMENT DEVELOPMENT

For any organization management development is a critical process. This process can be considered from two perspectives. The first is to identify high-flyers and the second is to facilitate their development. HR practitioners in the UK use a variety of tools to support the managerial development process (*see* Table 5.11). This is not the case in all European nations; in some countries HR practitioners may strongly prefer one tool over the next. Table 5.11, however, does not show much variation in the use of different tools between the UK and the EU. In fact the percentages are very similar, but there are actually varied country practices.

**TABLE 5.11**

**Management development tools (in % of organizations)**

|  | UK 1992 | 1999* | EU 1999 |
| --- | --- | --- | --- |
| Career plans | 34 | 32 | 32 |
| Assessment centres | 27 | 31 | 26 |
| Planned job rotation | 27 | 30 | 34 |
| High-flyer scheme for managers | 37 | 27 | 39 |
| International experience scheme for managers | 26 | 23 | 24 |

* 1995 data are not comparable with 1992 and 1999, due to question formulation

The UK results indicate that 32 per cent of practitioners use career plans. The results vary slightly by industry sector. Organizations in the public sector, for instance, are least likely to put in place career plans (21 per cent only), whereas organizations in business services are much more likely to do so (39 per cent).

Overall, the EU average is the same as the UK average. However, amongst European nations, career plans seem to be a preferred tool in southern Europe, e.g. Spain, Greece and Italy. Indeed, career plans have hardly been adopted in Finland and Sweden. On the whole, given the high rate of change in the environment, the majority of organizations are hard put to establish strict formal plans – regardless of the country. Hence this HR tool may not have the overwhelming salience it had a few decades ago.

As regards assessment/development centres, they are, despite their cost, increasingly being used by UK practitioners. Their use is by far the most preferred method of identifying and meeting development needs in the Netherlands, Finland, and Belgium (with respectively five, four, and three out of every ten organizations using them), followed by the UK. At the other end of the scale, Denmark, Portugal, Sweden and Ireland seem to disfavour using assessment centres, favouring a mixture of other tools, including succession plans.

French practitioners responding to the Cranet Survey indicate that they strongly favour planned job rotation (73 per cent) and high-flyer schemes (60 per cent). These results strongly contrast with the UK. The French were also less likely to use assessment centres, relying more on educational background as sufficient proof of ability, especially when the high potential managers are elite *grandes écoles* graduates. In France and Germany selection and development through assessment centres may be seen as disrespectful and unnecessary (Barsoux & Lawrence, 1997). This is because, in these countries, educational credentials are considered largely sufficient as a measure of achievement and potential.

## APPRAISAL

Employee appraisals are a key means of addressing training needs, but clearly this is not their sole purpose. In the UK the use of appraisals as a developmental tool is widespread, especially at the top of organizations.

The 1999 Cranet Survey shows that a majority of UK organizations use appraisals for all grades of staff. Indeed, appraisals are increasingly being used for manual and clerical staff, with the largest rise in these categories between 1995 and 1999 (*see* Table 5.12). Best-practice organizations would therefore extend appraisals to clerical and manual staff. One of the HR managers on the panel confirmed this trend: 'Appraisals are being pushed down our organization, including for secretarial and manual jobs. This was always in place, but now we make sure that it is no longer simply a formality but that it is carried out thoroughly.'

| | UK 1995 | 1999 | EU 1999 |
|---|---|---|---|
| Management | 90 | 92 | 72 |
| Professional/technical | 87 | 91 | 74 |
| Clerical | 76 | 86 | 67 |
| Manual | 51 | 69 | 57 |

**TABLE 5.12**

**Organizations using appraisal systems (in %)**

In fact, at managerial level, the system of appraisal is used in the UK more than in any other EU nation. Swedish organizations are just ahead of the UK in terms of spreading appraisals to all other categories of staff. The UK and Sweden are therefore models of best practice, in tune with today's flatter management structures. The use of appraisals is not as popular in all countries (e.g. Denmark, Finland and Germany). Yet even in these countries about one in two organizations will have an appraisal system in place.

The nature of appraisals can vary considerably. A critical question is who is involved. Traditionally, appraisals are carried out by an employee's immediate superior. In fact, this traditional pattern of boss and subordinates does predominate in the UK as well as in Europe (*see* Table 5.13). However, increasingly appraisals also take into account the view of the employee themselves, and that of the next-level superior. A few organizations go as far as carrying out full-circle appraisals, called 360-degree feedback, and involving peers, as well as subordinates, superiors and customers.

**TABLE 5.13**

**Involvement in appraisal systems (in % of organizations)**

|  | UK 1999 | EU 1999 |
|---|---|---|
| Immediate superior | 92 | 82 |
| Next-level superior | 57 | 43 |
| The employee | 88 | 50 |
| Subordinates | 11 | 7 |
| Peers | 11 | 6 |
| Customers | 9 | 8 |

This 360-degree feedback is considered best practice (*IRS Employment Trends*, 2000) as it is based on multiple viewpoints and therefore gives an assessment of someone's performance that is more encompassing than if it was based on the immediate superior only. However, 360-degree feedback requires a heavy involvement of the HR function, in terms of making sure confidentiality is assured, analyzing the organization's results and following through with organizational and personal development plans – so much so that only 4.3 per cent of organizations in the UK used the 360-degree assessment. This compares favourably with the 1995 Cranet results which showed that only 2.4 per cent of organizations used 360-degree feedback. More organizations are pioneering this technique but it has not been adopted by a significant majority. Other EU countries are even less likely to adopt 360-degree assessments.

The biggest difference between the UK and other EU nations is that in the EU the employees themselves are much less likely to have any input in their own appraisal. UK HR practitioners also differ from their continental colleagues in that they use appraisals for slightly different purposes (*see* Table 5.14).

TABLE 5.14

**Uses of appraisal systems (in % of organizations)**

|  | UK 1999 | EU 1999 |
|---|---|---|
| Individual training needs | 92 | 68 |
| Career development | 72 | 50 |
| Organizational training needs | 66 | 42 |
| Promotional potential | 58 | 54 |
| Organization of work | 40 | 34 |
| Individual performance-related pay | 31 | 45 |

In the UK the appraisal is mostly an occasion to review an employee's development. Hence it is an opportunity to talk in the first instance about individual training needs (92 per cent of cases) and in the second instance to talk about career development. UK HR practitioners also emphasize the fact that individual development is inextricably linked with organization development. The British view is that an organization cannot change and grow if employees do not develop.

Overall, in the EU appraisals are, as in the UK, an opportunity to discuss individual training needs. However, appraisals are also often used as a means of identifying promotion potential. The emphasis in the EU is therefore strongly placed on the individual, whereas UK organizations are more likely to consider the needs of the organization as a whole. However, Sweden does lead the UK in terms of taking on board the overall view of the organization, as opposed to focusing on individuals. Indeed, Swedish managers are more interested in using appraisals as a means of reviewing the organization of work and less concerned with individual development.

The appraisal system in the UK is least used for the purpose of determining performance-related pay. It is helpful to contrast the UK with the French model which presents the reverse situation. In France the appraisal system is used first and foremost to determine performance-related pay. One of the UK practitioners on the panel, commenting on these findings, pointed out that in their organization the results of appraisals were now published on the intranet, with individuals signing off their appraisals. There were mixed reactions to this change, which appeared to have turned the appraisal into a selling tool for individuals, so that the developmental purpose had been lost.

Summarizing these points, UK HR practitioners have overwhelmingly adopted appraisals, particularly for managers, but also increasingly for other categories of employees. These appraisals are mostly an occasion to map out individual training needs, career development and organizational development. The use of appraisals as a personal selling tool or a way of determining performance-related pay appears to be less welcome by UK organizations. A minority of organizations are getting smarter at integrating feedback from different levels of hierarchy and implementing 360-degree feedback. Such a system is heavy to manage from an HR perspective but the benefits can be significant: for individuals, it is a means of fostering personal development, for organizations, it is a means of measuring and reinforcing cultural change. Best practice may not dictate the systematic use of 360-degree feedback and seems to suggest that it works best when individuals volunteer for such a feedback. Finally, best practice does indicate that organizations that use appraisals in a formal manner, using mixed inputs, are most likely to see their employee-development strategies benefit.

> *"Appraisals are mostly an occasion to map out individual training needs, career development and organizational development"*

## CONCLUSION

The Cranet Survey offers many insights into employee development practices in the UK and other countries. Indeed, UK HR practitioners can learn from the many contrasts drawn from different industry sectors and EU nations. These differences in emphasis are revealing, yet the overall message across Europe, regardless of industry background, is that employee development is an essential component of the HR portfolio. It includes training but also personal development and, in the wider sense, the monitoring of individuals and of their performance in the organization. Best practice suggests that employee development stretches far beyond occasional training programmes, which may be subject to the positive or detrimental effect of an organization's financial results. In many ways, employee development is a joint-investment:

- employees have a vested interest in their personal development;
- organizations have a vested interest in developing a workforce capable of shaping the organization.

Training and development is not an isolated entity driven in an *ad hoc* manner by short-term business needs, nor is it a set of activities sponsored by philanthropic employers. It is at its most powerful when the individual needs of employees and the needs of the organization are effectively combined and aligned with strategic objectives.

## REFERENCES

Barsoux, J.L. & Lawrence, P. (1997) *French Management: Elitism in action*. London: Cassell.

Glover, I. & Hughes, M. (eds) (1996) *The Professional Managerial Class: Contemporary British management in the pursuer mode*. Aldershot: Ashgate.

*IRS Employment Trends* (2000) '360-degree feedback, a rounded view', (705), June, pp. 5–9.

Lane, C. (1989) *Management and Labour in Europe: The industrial enterprise in Germany, Britain and France*. Aldershot: Edward Elgar.

Lawrence, P. & Edwards, V. (2000) *Management in Western Europe*. London: Macmillan.

Pettinger, R. (1994) *Introduction to Management*. London: Macmillan.

Tregaskis, O. (1997) 'The role of national context and HR strategy in shaping training and development practice in French and UK organizations', *Organization Studies*, 18 (5), pp. 839–56.

Zander, L. (1999) 'Management in Sweden' in *The International Encyclopedia of Business and Management* (Europe volume). London: International Thomson Press.

# 6

## Compensation and benefits

## EXECUTIVE SUMMARY

In this chapter we look at the trends in the use of different systems of compensation and benefits for employees across Europe. Particularly we focus on the different systems of variable pay in operation that are designed to reward both individual and corporate performance over the short- and long-term, and on family-friendly benefits and pensions that support cash reward systems.

The main findings are:

- In the UK in the late 1990s the growth previously seen in the use of variable pay has been consolidated, and if anything has seen a small decline. It is not the same story across Europe, however, where an increase in the proportion of organizations using variable pay is generally more common.

- The share of organizations using performance-related pay fell in 1999 for the first time during the 1990s. This decline can be found across all sectors of industry.

- Group bonuses are remaining popular for management grades in the private sector; however, they continue to be more popular for manual grades in public-sector organizations.

- There is a higher use of employee share-option schemes than profit-sharing schemes in the UK, which stands in contrast to the European trend.

- The public sector remains three times as likely to offer non-pay benefits (as part of the reward package) as private-sector organizations.

- The use of family-friendly non-pay benefits in the UK does not appear to have been increasing in use as widely as other forms of non-pay benefit; if anything, they have been on the decline.

- The UK has a very high level of provision of pension schemes by employers compared across Europe.

- In general it is difficult to compare payment systems across national boundaries as schemes tend to be representative of national regulatory and statutory requirements, as well as cultural preferences.

## INTRODUCTION

During the last two decades the focus of compensation and benefit policies has shifted substantially in an attempt to align both corporate and individual performance. This shift reflects a number of social, political and economic changes, including the influence of Conservative governments, the decline in the strength of trade unions, and high levels of unemployment in some sectors with skill shortages developing in others. Commentators were also noting a change in the social environment, with employees demanding individual salary increases, and the introduction of variability in pay rewards and performance-related pay. UK organizations were increasingly focusing on augmenting the level of reward available to high achievers. This was resulting in an associated rise in the use of flexible pay and benefit schemes by employers. At the macro-level the business environment had been changing rapidly, and employers were under pressure to control reward strategies.

These changes were taking place on two dimensions: a rise in personal performance as a criterion for reward determination, and a change in the level at which reward policy is decided. Two decades ago most organizations were involved in industry-wide collective bargaining. Typical pay systems involved a series of progression elements. In this environment line managers generally did not have to deal with pay issues. The decline in industry-wide bargaining and the increased emphasis on individual performance have changed this. This has required a refocusing of management skills, and a shift in emphasis of the support provided by the HR department within organizations.

However, while arguably the same broad trends towards more diversified pay packages can be found in much of Europe, there is little sign of conversion in the ways in which this is implemented.

## VARIABLE PAY

A wide range of flexible remuneration benefits based on both individual and corporate performance form the whole package of variable pay that organizations have available to reward their employees. These include such schemes as performance-related pay, group bonuses, employee share options and profit sharing. Organizations have been under pressure to increase the scope of the reward package, particularly in line with cyclical trends related to labour market shortages.

However, towards the end of the decade the survey shows that this trend has been slowing down. In 1999 one in five organizations (22 per cent) in the UK did not operate a variable pay scheme. Of those who did, just over a quarter (28 per cent) reported an increase in the scheme's use over the last three years, and one in 20 (5 per cent) reported a decrease. Compared to previous years, this shows a consolidation in the use of variable pay. In 1990 over five out of ten (51 per cent) organizations had reported an increase in their use of variable pay over the previous three years. In 1992 this figure dropped to four out of ten (40 per cent) organizations. In 1995 this dropped again to less than one in three organizations (29 per cent).

If we look across industry sectors, the largest increase in the use of variable pay schemes has occurred in the private sector, where they are already used most widely (*see* Table 6.1). These figures emphasize how the public sector is lagging behind its private counterparts in introducing variable pay schemes, with one third (32 per cent) of public-sector organizations not having any variable pay schemes in place for their employees. It is likely that the public sector has been slower to move in this area due to the degree of unionization and centralized control within the organizational structures, although such speculation would need further investigation.

|  | UK 1999 Manufac- turing | Other industry | Business services | Other services | Public sector | UK average | EU 1999 EU average |
|---|---|---|---|---|---|---|---|
| Increase | 33 | 40 | 48 | 29 | 10 | 28 | 45 |
| Same | 42 | 48 | 41 | 45 | 53 | 45 | 37 |
| Decrease | 6 | 0 | 0 | 4 | 5 | 5 | 6 |
| Not used | 19 | 12 | 11 | 22 | 32 | 22 | 12 |

**TABLE 6.1**

**The use of variable pay schemes by sector (in % of organizations)**

Looking further afield, employers across Europe have generally been moving away from more rigid pay structures and increasing their use of variable pay. When viewed on this scale, the UK contrasts with many other countries in that its proportion of organizations increasing their use of variable pay schemes is the lowest in Europe (28 per cent). By direct contrast, the highest proportion of organizations increasing their use of variable pay schemes can be found in Italy and Spain, where the rate of increase is more than twice as high (61 per cent and 64 per cent respectively). These variations in the coverage of variable pay can result from a number of factors, including differences in pay-bargaining structures (how much freedom individual organizations have to set their own pay schemes) and in skill availability in the labour market (to what extent an individual can demand a certain reward package) (Filella & Hegewisch, 1994).

Although in general it is clear that variable pay schemes are in wide use, the executive director of a large UK-owned fashion retailer has recognized that the road is not an easy one to follow. He describes variable pay schemes as a 'hurdle of complexity', particularly when trying to work with group reward. How can you demonstrate how the different parts of the group interlink? Is there one bonus for the product, one for the brand, one for the sector, one for profit, etc?

As the use of variable pay schemes has become more sophisticated, other new forms of schemes have been appearing, such as team-based pay, competency-based pay and profit-related pay schemes. Although this survey has not specifically looked at these new schemes, there is evidence of their use appearing in a small but growing number of organizations.

Competency-based pay, for example, claims to address some of the inadequacies of performance-related pay by measuring individual performance relative to a set of valued competencies rather than against a set of targets that were agreed 12 months previously. This approach also goes hand-in-hand with the increasing focus on staff development within organizations as employees are recognized as the organization's source of competitive advantage and efficiency (Cira & Benjamin, 1998). Competency-based pay is particularly being used for manual-level employees and for those working in customer-service roles. It was reported as being used by 28 per cent of organizations in the UK in the 1999 CBI Employment Trends Survey.

The use of these schemes and other new variations and developments looks set to increase, particularly in certain areas of the labour market where there are skills shortages. The close links between reward packages and state regulation also mean that changes will continue as government policies come in and out of fashion.

## INCENTIVE SCHEMES

How do employers encourage each of their individual employees to reach a level of performance that will enable the organization to achieve its goals? Not many (if any) managers have the time, opportunity or inclination to walk around their organization every day, checking everyone is happy in their work and ironing out any problems that may be present.

It is likely that not all employees would appreciate this paternalistic approach anyway. So can we rely on pay-based approaches to motivation instead? Can we encourage staff performance through incentive schemes that reward hard work, loyalty, excellence and expertise? According to management theories of motivation we can certainly use such schemes as tools to help us towards this goal; pay can be instrumental for the satisfaction of both esteem and physiological needs (Lawler 1971).

One of the longest standing incentive schemes found in our workplaces today is that of individual payment by results, also known as piecework. However, over recent decades its use has declined as more sophisticated reward schemes have been implemented, emphasizing not only speed and quantity, but also the importance of quality. As the focus shifted towards monitoring behaviour rather than output, this led to the rise in popularity of merit or performance-related pay (PRP) throughout the 1980s. The spread in PRP relates both to the numbers of people involved and to the range of grades that it covered, extending from managerial to non-manual grades and indeed some manual grades as well (Cannell & Wood, 1992).

One key feature of these new pay schemes is that their introduction in the public sector has been markedly slower than in the private sector. At the start of a new decade, it now appears that there is change afoot again in flexible remuneration practices; just as UK teachers are being strongly encouraged to embrace PRP, the survey shows that there has been a clear drop in its use across both public- and private-sector organizations.

## Performance-related pay

The use of PRP as a short-term incentive reward scheme has traditionally been reserved for managers in the private sector. It represented a change in thinking when it was first introduced, switching from structures of job grading to individual performance grading. Despite its rise to glory in the late 1980s, the use of merit or performance-related pay for managerial and professional grades declined considerably over the past five years (*see* Table 6.2). We could speculate about the reasons for this unexpected decline in its use. Individual performance-related pay is particularly effective in times of competitive expansion, encouraging individuals to outperform their colleagues and, as a result, to take home the largest pay packets (IDS, 1988). This has inflationary effects on wage systems, which increases the expectations of all employees. If an organization's performance is plateauing after a period of successful growth, it will find it difficult to limit

*"More sophisticated reward schemes have been implemented, emphasizing not only speed and quantity, but also the importance of quality"*

the level of pay rises and who receives them. The end of the last decade has been associated more so with consolidation of economic activity, and as such this may be contributing to this decline in PRP recorded in the survey. It will be interesting to see in the next round of the survey in three years time whether this same trend is still discernable.

**TABLE 6.2**

Merit/performance-related pay use by grade (in % of organizations)

|  | UK 1990 | 1992 | 1995 | 1999 | EU 1999 |
|---|---|---|---|---|---|
| Management | 65 | 65 | 64 | 49 | 47 |
| Professional | 56 | 52 | 48 | 40 | 45 |
| Clerical | 44 | 42 | 39 | 33 | 37 |
| Manual | 23 | 21 | 22 | 22 | 28 |

Looking closer at the usage of PRP by sector we can clearly see the distinction between the public and private sectors (*see* Table 6.3). Particularly for managerial grades, organizations in the private sector are around twice as likely to have a PRP scheme in place for their staff than those in the public sector.

**TABLE 6.3**

Merit/performance-related pay use by grade and sector (in % of organizations)

|  | UK 1999 Manufac- turing | Other industry | Business services | Other services | Public sector | UK average | EU 1999 EU average |
|---|---|---|---|---|---|---|---|
| Management | 56 | 49 | 69 | 48 | 30 | 49 | 47 |
| Professional | 44 | 42 | 66 | 43 | 17 | 40 | 45 |
| Clerical | 34 | 33 | 58 | 38 | 15 | 33 | 37 |
| Manual | 22 | 21 | 24 | 32 | 13 | 22 | 28 |

If we focus our attention wider, differences can be seen across Europe in the use of PRP for managerial grades, with an increase over the last decade in Sweden (from 12 to 20 per cent), compared to the decline in use in the UK (from 65 to 49 per cent). It is noteworthy, though, that some countries across Europe, such as Germany, do not use PRP predominantly for managerial grades, but have a wider coverage for manual grades. This is compensated by German organizations making much wider use instead of corporate profit sharing for managerial grades, as we shall see in the following sections. In Sweden the use of PRP is low for all grades of staff, and in France it is high for all grades, showing how each country has its own cultural preference for attracting, rewarding and retaining its employees. For example, the heavy reliance on PRP in France can be explained by the relevant legal and fiscal regulations. In Scandinavian countries it is generally individually negotiated pay that predominates rather than individual or organizational PRP; this raises the question of what criteria are being used to decide salary levels in these countries.

One HR director at a major international petroleum company found the fall in the use of PRP in the UK astonishing, stating that this certainly did not reflect practice in his organization. Could this perhaps be a change in how schemes are being devised and run rather than a real move away from PRP? However, the reaction of the manager for information, pay and standards at one county council is less surprised: 'We have dropped PRP for higher managers and have replaced it with fixed-term contracts [as a means of controlling performance]. The reasons are the costs of PRP; school heads felt that money really should be spent on essentials instead, such as books or roofs!'

## Group bonus schemes

With the rise in the late 1980s of management techniques such as Total Quality Management, commentators were beginning to promote the belief that achieving total quality depended on a team approach (Edwards, 1988). Schemes of group payment by results or group bonuses paid to a whole group or team on the basis of pre-arranged productivity targets were becoming increasingly popular.

Unlike PRP, the use of group bonus schemes has remained relatively constant throughout the last decade. Today, as with PRP, group bonus schemes are also found more commonly in the private sector (*see* Table 6.4). One interesting point to note is that the use of these schemes is most popular for managers and least popular for manual staff in the private sector, whilst the opposite is true in the public sector.

| | UK 1999 Manufacturing | Other industry | Business services | Other services | Public sector | UK average | EU 1999 EU average |
|---|---|---|---|---|---|---|---|
| Management | 44 | 36 | 50 | 34 | 5 | 32 | 15 |
| Professional | 26 | 36 | 45 | 22 | 6 | 24 | 16 |
| Clerical | 23 | 27 | 40 | 18 | 6 | 20 | 15 |
| Manual | 22 | 32 | 21 | 15 | 16 | 19 | 17 |

**TABLE 6.4**

**Group bonus scheme use by sector and grade (in % of organizations)**

In general, the application of group bonus schemes remains relatively limited in the UK, particularly for non-managerial grades and public-sector organizations. This may be due to the difficulties of operating such a scheme in practice and a general preference for schemes related to individual performance. One organization that is an exception to this is Shell International: from 1995 to 1999 its policy changed from almost no one receiving a team bonus to almost everyone. In this case the definition of a team varies: sometimes it can cover all 3000 people in a group, for example, on health and safety targets or quality; sometimes it involves smaller teams of just ten people.

This raises one of the key issues of group-bonus reward schemes. Increasingly 'team reward' is being used in a much more corporate sense, trying to focus employees' attention on the overall group/company performance and strategy. This is spreading its use from the more obvious small project team to the much larger group of employees involving whole divisions. Because of this lack of distinction, it is difficult to compare practices with other European countries, as the idea of a group is interpreted in many different ways. Indeed, pay remains one of the areas of HRM practices most strongly affected by national differences (Filella & Hegewisch, 1994).

*"HR departments become a source of invaluable information to link individual and group efforts to corporate objectives"*

In general, how effective these reward schemes are at actually incentivizing employees is a matter for debate, and is obviously related to organizational and indeed national culture. However, one thing is clear: wherever these schemes are operating, the responsibility to manage the schemes lies with management, and hence reinforces the organizational hierarchy. Performance management becomes a key skill for line management if equitable remuneration and the desired level of motivation are to be achieved. HR departments then become a source of invaluable information to maintain relativities in pay and benefits and to link individual and group efforts to corporate objectives.

## Financial involvement

A more long-term approach to employee motivation and reward, and one that focuses on the individual's contribution to organizational performance, is the use of employee share-option schemes and profit sharing. With the stimulus of government taxation incentives, these methods of rewarding employees were being introduced just over a decade ago. Both mechanisms offer a degree of wage flexibility with a low basic wage plus a percentage per capita of profit that can ensure constancy through economic cycles. Hence the government's keenness to support such schemes during times of economic uncertainty, and to encourage the development of an enterprise culture.

Managerial grades are again the most likely group of staff to be offered such schemes (*see* Table 6.5). In the 1990s the use of employee share options has seen a small decline (between 7 and 10 per cent depending on the grade of staff). Profit sharing has slightly lower coverage than share-option schemes amongst managerial staff (a third of organizations in 1999 used employee share option schemes for managerial staff, compared to a quarter using profit sharing). For all grades the use of profit sharing is little different today than it was at the beginning of the last decade, a finding which is also supported by the 1998 Workplace Employee Relations Survey in the UK (Millward *et al*, 2000).

| Share options | UK 1990 | 1992 | 1995 | 1999 | EU 1999 |
|---|---|---|---|---|---|
| Management | 42 | 37 | 31 | 32 | 20 |
| Professional | 31 | 29 | 22 | 23 | 11 |
| Clerical | 27 | 25 | 19 | 20 | 10 |
| Manual | 24 | 22 | 17 | 17 | 8 |
| Profit sharing | UK 1990 | 1992 | 1995 | 1999 | EU 1999 |
| Management | 29 | 26 | 27 | 24 | 40 |
| Professional | 23 | 21 | 23 | 22 | 29 |
| Clerical | 21 | 19 | 22 | 21 | 25 |
| Manual | 17 | 17 | 19 | 18 | 20 |

**TABLE 6.5**

**The use of employee share options and profit sharing by grade (in % of organizations)**

In the early 1990s the European Commission was seeking to intervene in patterns of financial participation in all EU member countries. By adopting a recommendation to encourage member states to promote and facilitate financial participation by employees, and suggesting core criteria and issues to consider when setting up such schemes, the Commission was trying to influence share-ownership schemes and profit sharing through recommendations on legal and tax incentives. Such approaches, and indeed the approaches currently under discussion in the UK, have a strong egalitarian component: tax incentives are dependent on having schemes that are open to all employee groups. However, the access to such schemes remains rather hierarchical and the overall take-up rate of such schemes still remains relatively low across Europe. The EU average for employee share-option schemes is 20 per cent of organizations for managerial grades and 8 per cent for manual grades, and for profit-sharing schemes 40 per cent for management and 20 per cent for manual staff (*see* Table 6.5).

Looking at individual countries, there are again some interesting variations in the average figures, emphasizing the importance of national culture and institutions in how we reward our employees. In the Nordic countries both share-option and profit-sharing schemes are, and have been, unpopular, for all staff groups. Such types of incentives continue to be perceived as inappropriate. The UK trend shows a preference for share-option schemes to profit sharing while in Germany the reverse is true. France has a high uptake of profit-sharing schemes across all grades of staff, due to legislative requirements.

## EMPLOYEE BENEFITS

Clearly, in terms of non-pay benefits for employees, there are many schemes ranging from company cars to private health care plans. Here we highlight trends in the two areas covered by the survey, selected due to particular policy interests: family-friendly benefits and company pension schemes.

### Family-friendly benefits

Workplace childcare, childcare allowances, career-break schemes and maternity and paternity leave became increasingly popular in the 1970s when labour-market shortages forced employers to increase their attempts to attract and retain female employees. Since then they have become an accepted part of our reward packages, and continue to be an important complementary tool in recruitment and retention policies.

In 1999 in the UK almost a quarter of organizations (21 per cent) reported an increase in the use of family-friendly benefit schemes over the last three years and only 6 per cent a decrease. However, despite these reported increases, in terms of offering family-friendly non-pay benefits above those required by law, there has been a slight reduction over the last five years in the total number of organizations offering such schemes. Career-break schemes are the only family-friendly non-pay benefit schemes that have seen an increased level of usage during the second half of the 1990s, be it only a small increase of 2 per cent of organizations. Given that we saw in Chapter 3 that the UK is leading the way in Europe in terms of policies for equal opportunities in employment, this is quite a remarkable finding.

The split between public- and private-sector organizations in the use of non-pay benefits is also noteworthy. In 1999 public-sector organizations were around three times as likely to offer such non-pay benefits as organizations in the private sector (*see* Table 6.6). It could be argued that this higher-than-average level of provision of non-pay benefits perhaps compensates for the lack of variable pay schemes in the sector.

**TABLE 6.6**

**The use of non-pay benefit schemes by sector (in % of organizations)**

| | UK 1999 Manufac- turing | Other industry | Business services | Other services | Public sector | UK average | EU 1999 EU average |
|---|---|---|---|---|---|---|---|
| Workplace childcare | 1 | 9 | 9 | 7 | 33 | 12 | 6 |
| Childcare allowances | 3 | 7 | 6 | 5 | 9 | 5 | 13 |
| Career-break schemes | 6 | 23 | 22 | 15 | 47 | 21 | 19 |
| Maternity leave | 29 | 39 | 40 | 42 | 89 | 49 | 26 |
| Paternity leave | 27 | 36 | 40 | 37 | 68 | 41 | 22 |

If we compare the UK with the rest of Europe, we can see that the UK has relatively wide usage of such benefits that are in the main aimed at working parents. However, in many regards this also reflects lower public provision – employers have to make up for the lack of publicly provided childcare for example. And given that in most EU countries the rights of fathers are considerably better established in law than in the UK, it is not surprising that most UK employers do not offer more than what is required by statute. There are other interesting differences. In the UK the term 'career break' is firmly linked to working women taking a break to have children, even though there is a growing number of people – men and women – who want to take time out for educational or other personal reasons. In France it is this second conception that defines the term, and indeed employees have the legal right to a leave of absence from their job for educational purposes.

More generally, the popularity of non-pay benefits in different countries is heavily influenced by their tax effectiveness and the cultural expectations of the local workforce. In general it is the Anglo-Germanic countries that have a more balanced reward package between financial and non-financial rewards, whereas the Latin and Scandinavian countries favour a more biased financial package. In support of this, French organizations are particularly reticent in using non-pay benefit schemes, since there is a known preference for hard cash in the French reward culture. Belgium has seen the highest level of increase over recent years, with 40 per cent of organizations increasing their use of non-pay benefits, compared to Sweden's level of 7 per cent, the lowest in Europe.

One approach to offering employees non-pay benefits is through a flexible 'cafeteria' benefits scheme. Flexible benefits schemes allow staff to trade some of the benefits in their basic package for extra cash, holidays, health insurance, childcare vouchers, etc. For example, one of the major banks in the UK has introduced a flexible benefits scheme as a means of developing a competitive edge in a tight labour market. A flexible benefits scheme is also seen as a better way of rewarding all staff rather than taking a more paternalistic approach (Blackman, 1999). These schemes are linked to improving motivation, performance and other flexible working arrangements: during times of low inflation, when cash pay rises are limited, non-pay items give a competitive edge. This trend looks set to continue. Around half of the organizations surveyed in a recent study by Towers Perrin across Europe were planning to introduce a wider choice of benefits, with the UK leading the way (Brown, 1999). However, in 1995, the last time we surveyed organizations on this point, only 14 per cent of organizations operated a cafeteria benefits scheme, showing just how recent and quick these changes have been.

## Pensions

Recent years have seen many changes in pension provision, due to the changing nature of the work environment. First, employees do not expect to keep the same job for life. Second, given current demographics, the government's pension provision, which is based on today's workers paying for today's pensioners, will not be financially viable in the very near future. A further issue lies in the increasing use of flexible working practices (discussed in Chapter 4): short-term contract workers are rarely included in pension schemes or other fringe benefits. The range of flexible working patterns – including career breaks, part-time and short-contract working – also interrupt the period over which an individual contributes to the pension fund. Women workers currently make up almost half of the workforce and are of particular concern, as they form the group most likely to take time out between jobs to care for a family. Given the recent activities of downsizing and right-sizing organizations, in 1999, 44 per cent of organizations said they reduced their workforce through early retirement, again putting pressure on pension funds.

It has been recognized that this lack of occupational pension provision for many atypical workers will throw additional burdens on the state in years to come. Consequently, changes are currently being made in the law regarding the provision of pension schemes by all employers, including smaller organizations, which tend to be the poorest at offering such schemes. These changes in demographics and ways of working have already created new forms of pension schemes introduced through legislation, such as personal pensions and additional voluntary contributions. In the UK, in 1999, 95 per cent of organizations employing over 200 employees offered pension schemes. This proportion is equally represented across sectors. Compared with the rest of Europe this proportion of organizations is very high. In France the proportion is as low as 39 per cent, predominantly due to social provision and regulations.

*"Flexible remuneration and benefit schemes are still a substantial element of reward strategy in the UK"*

## CONCLUSIONS

The survey evidence shows that flexible remuneration and benefit schemes are still a substantial element of reward strategy in the UK, although their use is perhaps plateauing, if not declining, compared to a continued increase taking place across Europe on average.

Looking at specific examples in the UK of different forms of reward packages, we see that the use of share-option schemes has been high but is now declining slightly, whilst the use of profit sharing, which has narrower coverage, is remaining constant. Both schemes are predominantly being offered to managerial grades. The same is also true of group bonus schemes in the private sector, however, these schemes are more often used for manual grades in the public sector. The most noteworthy decline in flexible payment methods over this decade has been in the use of merit or performance-related pay; an interesting finding given the significance of this form of reward just a decade ago.

Distinctions remain clear in the use of different reward packages in the public compared to the private sector. In particular, the evidence of less general use of variable pay in the public sector is contrasted by more use of non-pay benefits as compared to the private sector. In general, however, family-friendly non-pay benefits do not appear to have been increasing in use as widely as other forms of non-pay benefits, and if anything have also been on the decline.

If we look at pension scheme provision by employers, the UK has an exceptionally high level of provision compared with the rest of Europe. In general this variation between countries shows how different patterns of variable pay and non-pay benefits are being used according to national legislative requirements and tax incentives, as well as in response to cultural demands from employers and employees. This has been demonstrated a number of times in this discussion on compensation issues. Although working on the same principles of wanting to recruit and retain high-quality staff, national context plays a significant role in this area of management practice.

## REFERENCES

Blackman, T. (1999) 'Trading in options', *People Management*, 5 (9), pp. 42–6.

Brown, D. (1999) 'States of pay', *People Management*, 5 (23), pp. 52–3.

Cannell, M. & Wood, S. (1992) *Incentive Pay: impact and evolution*. London: IPM/NEDO.

Cira, D.J. & Benjamin, E.R. (1998) 'Competency-based pay: a concept in evolution', *Compensation and Benefits Review*, 30 (5), pp. 21–8.

Edwards, D.W. (1988) *Out of the Crisis*. Cambridge: Cambridge University Press.

Filella, J. and Hegewisch, A. (1994) 'European experiments with pay and benefits policies' in C. Brewster and A. Hegewisch (eds) *Policy and Practice in European Human Resource Management* (pp. 89–106). London: Routledge.

IDS (1988) *Performance Pay*. (IDS Focus 49). London: Incomes Data Services.

Lawler, E.E. Jnr (1971) *Pay and Organizational Effectiveness*. New York: McGraw-Hill.

Millward, N., Bryson, A. & Forth, J. (2000) *All Change at Work?* London: Routledge.

# Employee
# communication

## EXECUTIVE SUMMARY

- There is little employment statute governing employee information, consultation and participation in the UK. What, how and whether UK employers communicate to their employees is largely left up to the individual organization (subject, of course, to any collective agreements). This makes the UK, with Ireland, comparatively unique in Europe. The high profile of rights to information and consultation in EU social policy gives further poignancy to this area of employee relation.

- Throughout the 1990s the large majority of UK organizations reported an increase in verbal and written communication to employees. While one might expect an equivalence between changes in downward and upward communication, on the whole the growth in communication from employees to management has been much more modest than that from management to employees. The exception is team briefings.

- The use of e-mail in employee communication has increased dramatically between 1995 and 1999. Particularly in financial and business services this is an omnipresent and expanding means of employee communication. Other sectors are still lagging behind. How far this explosion is beneficial, or highlights a need for information management rather than information overload, remains to be seen.

- On most indicators the growth in individual communication has been more dynamic in the UK than in other European countries. A north–south divide is apparent for some channels of communication, for example in the extent to which senior managers are seen as appropriate respondents in upward communication.

- Collective channels of communication have not been part of the communication explosion. At the same time, the large majority of UK organizations continue to use trade union and other collective channels for communication. The Cranet Survey, however, suggests that union influence and the role of unions in employee communications is no longer in overall decline and, at least in some sectors, has started to grow again.

- Three times as many UK employers do without collective communication channels as the EU average. That said, in most countries, as in the UK, developments in individual communication have outpaced those in collective employee communication.

- Much recent organizational change has been aimed at making organizations flatter and less hierarchical. Yet the Cranet data shows a strong continuing hierarchy in access to information on strategic issues and financial performance.

- On average, UK organizations are more likely to include all employees in strategic and financial information than other European employers. Looking at individual countries there is once again a strong north–south divide: Nordic countries generally are much more confident that they reach all employees than other employers, whereas hierarchies are rather steep in the Mediterranean countries, including France.

## INTRODUCTION

Good communication is at the core of good human resource management. If employers wish to secure employee commitment they have to gain their workforces' acceptance of change and ideally their positive and enthusiastic support for new organizational goals. A more fluid and change-driven environment increases the need for effective information exchange to give employees the context and tools in which to work. If employers want to benefit from the insight and creativity of employees, they must listen and have good upward channels of communication. This is especially so where job roles have grown and where employees are asked to exert more autonomy of judgement.

The pressures for improved employee communication within Europe are universal. The same cannot be said about the ways in which organizations handle communication. Employee communication encompasses a myriad of channels and approaches, from genuine two-way exchanges and participation in decision making with team briefings or quality circles, to one-way communication via corporate newsletters or notice-boards. With the exception of some statutory obligations on, for example, the provision of information on health and safety, redundancies, pensions and individual terms and conditions, it is largely up to UK companies themselves to define the nature and extent of employee communication. Whether or not organizations pass on information, and whether and how they consult about work-related or business decisions, is largely up to management (subject, of course, to collective agreements, which continue to be in place in the majority of larger employers).

Such a voluntarist approach to information, consultation and participation makes the UK, and Ireland, unique in the EU. Elsewhere there is a much greater degree of statutory regulation. Employee communication, moreover, is an important part in EU social policy. Further rights to information and consultation were part of a quid pro quo to gain the consensus of working people and trade unions for the far-reaching economic changes in the wake of the introduction of the single European market. The new rights, introduced through the European Treaties, for consultation in European companies add an international layer of statute on employee relations to already comparatively well-developed national frameworks.

This chapter reviews:

- UK and European trends in downward and upward communication, including the use of team briefings, electronic mail and attitude surveys;

- the changing role of trade unions in communication;

- the extent to which organizations pass on strategic and financial information;

- how inclusive organizations are in their communications policies (and whether the move towards flatter organizational structures is matched by less hierarchical communication practices).

## DOWNWARD COMMUNICATION – FROM MANAGEMENT TO EMPLOYEES

The last decade has seen an explosion in direct employee communication. In each year of the Cranet research a minimum of six out of ten organizations report an increase in the volume of direct verbal communication from management to employees and the growth in written communication is not far behind (*see* Table 7.1). The data shows remarkable consistency in these trends across all sectors of the UK economy (*see* Table 7.2). There are a number of possible reasons for this. Organizations are much more concerned to present a coherent picture to the outside world and ensure that employees are aware of, if not share, the organization's basic values. Flatter organizational structures have facilitated more informal communication at the lower levels of organizations. Quality initiatives generally require an increased flow of information on workplace issues to relevant teams and workers, as does the general widening of job roles. If employees are to exert greater autonomy and responsibility in their jobs, they need to have access to a wider range of information. Last but not least, the rise in general levels of education and shift towards more knowledge-intensive production has arguably increased the demand for information and communication from employees who want to be more involved and consulted about their work.

**TABLE 7.1**

Increase in downward communication over time (in % of organizations)

|  | UK 1991 | 1992 | 1995 | 1999 | EU 1999 |
|---|---|---|---|---|---|
| Direct verbal | 65 | 63 | 63 | 62 | 47 |
| Written | 61 | 59 | 62 | 59 | 45 |
| Team briefings | n/a | n/a | 55 | 59 | 44 |
| E-mail | n/a | n/a | 39 | 73 | 67 |

**TABLE 7.2**

Increase in downward communication by sector (in % of organizations)

|  | UK 1999 Manufacturing | Other industry | Business services | Other services | Public sector |
|---|---|---|---|---|---|
| Direct verbal | 69 | 68 | 63 | 58 | 65 |
| Written | 60 | 56 | 64 | 61 | 66 |
| Team briefings | 59 | 54 | 58 | 60 | 58 |
| E-mail | 68 | 85 | 86 | 75 | 70 |

Direct communication to employees occurs through a variety of channels, from newsletters and videos, to meetings with the workforce, to informal reliance on line managers. Besides direct written and verbal means, our research focused on two particular channels for management to get their message across: team briefings and electronic mail. Team briefings are by now a well-established component of communication processes. Nine out of ten organizations use team briefings in at least part of the organization, a figure that has changed little since the mid 1990s.[1] Almost 60 per cent of organizations report an increase in the role of team briefings, by making them more central in communication processes or by introducing them to broader sections of the workforce (*see* Tables 7.1 and 7.2).

---

1  The 1998 Workplace Employee Relations Survey (WERS) suggests a lower use of team briefings in only 45 per cent of the surveyed workplaces (Cully *et al*, 1999). This discrepancy is likely to be due to differences in the survey design: the Cranet Survey addresses organizations centrally, whereas the WERS analyzes workplaces with a maximum of 25 employees. An organization responding to the Cranet Survey might well consist of several workplaces covered by WERS, some of which might have team briefings, others not.

While team briefings are already part of the established canon of communication, the use of e-mails is more novel. Between 1995 and 1999 the share of organizations using e-mail as part of their employee communication strategy has increased dramatically from less than 60 to more than 80 per cent. This is an area with clear leaders and laggards and continued strong sector differences, even though these have evened out considerably. Financial and business services are leading the trend towards e-mail; less than 5 per cent of companies in this sector do not use e-mail-based employee communication (down from 25 per cent only four years earlier). Not only is e-mail almost universally used in this sector, it also has the highest share – 85 per cent – of organizations having increased the use of e-mail as part of their written employee communication (*see* Table 7.2). How far this explosion is beneficial, or is highlighting a need for information management rather than information overload, remains to be seen. The sectoral laggard is the public sector, which has the lowest take-up, with one in five organizations stating that e-mail is not used for employee communication.

*"Employee involvement means giving employees a voice in the way that work is organized"*

## UPWARD COMMUNICATION – FROM EMPLOYEES TO MANAGEMENT

Upward communication, from employees to management, should be as important as downward communication. Employee involvement means giving employees a voice in the way that work is organized. The knowledge economy relies on utilizing the brains and creativity of employees to develop organizations' competitive edge and ensure an effective use of resources. Improvements in service quality need rapid feedback from those with a direct client interface. Furthermore, in all organizations, motivation, commitment and, not least, retention require employers to be aware of the issues and concerns of the workforce. Hence one would expect there to be as much pressure for an expansion in upward as in downward communication. On the whole, however, the data does not confirm this; the growth in upward communication has been much more modest than that in communication from management to employees. Organizations rely on a variety of channels. With the exception of team briefings, which have seen an increase corresponding to their use in downward communication, on average about a third of organizations report an increase in the different channels (*see* Table 7.3).

**TABLE 7.3**

**Increase and non-use in channels of upward communication over time (in % of organizations)**

| | UK 1992 (Yes/No)* | 1995 | 1999 | EU 1999 |
|---|---|---|---|---|
| **Direct to senior managers:** | | | | |
| increased | n/a | 34 | 34 | 26 |
| not used | 3 | 3 | 3 | 7 |
| **Line managers:** | | | | |
| increased | n/a | 31 | 32 | 29 |
| not used | 0 | 0 | 0 | 0 |
| **Workforce meetings:** | | | | |
| increased | n/a | 33 | 34 | 22 |
| not used | 31 | 19 | 17 | 10 |
| **Team briefings:** | | | | |
| increased | n/a | 49 | 49 | 35 |
| not used | n/a | 13 | 11 | 15 |
| **Suggestion schemes:** | | | | |
| increased | n/a | 21 | 17 | 18 |
| not used | 57 | 46 | 44 | 48 |
| **Attitude surveys:** | | | | |
| increased | n/a | 37 | 31 | 24 |
| not used | 54 | 41 | 43 | 43 |

\* The relevant questions in the survey changed since 1992: in 1992 there was no question about changes in upward communication

Line managers are seen as the basic element in communication – virtually no organization claims that they do not have a say in downward communication. Senior managers are almost as likely to be seen as a channel for upward communication, even though open-door policies and communication directly to senior management have had a mixed press – being welcomed as a sign of less hierarchical and more open management on the one hand but on the other potentially undermining middle management. About a third of organizations have increased the role of senior management in upward communication. There has also been a significant growth in the use of general workforce meetings. These meetings are used in 83 per cent of organizations and have been used more extensively in a third of organizations, especially in larger employers, particularly in the public sector (see Table 7.4)

Suggestion schemes are probably not the most sophisticated means of engaging employees but they are a long-established method of employee involvement and communications. Although they fell out of fashion, they have come back into favour because of Total Quality Management, continuous improvement (kaizen), team-working and similar schemes designed to make use of employees' potential for innovation and creativity.

Suggestion schemes are used by slightly over half of organizations, and are being made greater use of particularly in organizations in public and private services (*see* Table 7.4.)

| | UK 1999 Manufacturing | Other industry | Business services | Other services | Public sector |
|---|---|---|---|---|---|
| Direct to senior management | 35 | 42 | 40 | 30 | 36 |
| Line managers | 36 | 30 | 36 | 28 | 30 |
| Workforce meetings | 37 | 35 | 33 | 29 | 39 |
| Team briefings | 52 | 44 | 43 | 53 | 53 |
| Suggestion schemes | 18 | 12 | 19 | 21 | 21 |
| Attitude surveys | 30 | 31 | 43 | 33 | 35 |

**TABLE 7.4**

**Increase in channels of upward communication by sector (in % of organizations)**

There also has been a growth in the use of attitude surveys. There are a number of reasons for organizations to pay greater attention to employee views. The increase in labour-market fluidity – the challenge to traditional notions of career development and long-term attachment to an employer – has thrown into sharp relief the mutual expectations between employer and employees. Apart from general concerns about the changing 'psychological contract', there are now a number of good-practice management models, such as the one by the European Foundation for Quality, which include measures of employee motivation and attitudes as part of corporate performance measurement. As representative channels of communication have declined, employers also have had to pay more attention to developing alternative ways of assessing attitudes of the workforce, and attitude surveys are one way of systematically collecting information from employees. Hence it is not surprising that there has been an increased reliance on attitude surveys. Particularly larger employers are making use of attitude surveys: almost eight out of ten employers with more than 5000 employees use attitude surveys, and over half in this group have increased their use; less than a third of employers with less than 1000 employees have seen similar trends, and less than half of this group use attitude surveys.

## European trends in individual employee communication

On most indicators the growth in individual employee communication has been more dynamic in the UK than in Europe overall. This is not simply a result of averaging out European trends; generally UK developments exceed those in most countries. Other countries that have seen comparable growth in individual employee communication are Belgium, Ireland and Italy. In relation to some channels, especially workforce meetings and attitude surveys, less growth may be an indication of a more established and traditional use of these channels. Thus less than 5 per cent of German organizations report greater use of workforce meetings, but then these are in any case obligatory for most German organizations. Attitude surveys, on the other hand, are much more widely used in the Nordic countries.

Interesting differences also exist in relation to the role of senior managers in upward communication. In Spain the share of organizations reporting that senior managers are not seen as a channel for gathering employee views exceeds 15 per cent, and in France, Greece and Portugal this proportion exceeds 10 per cent, compared to a Nordic average of under 3 per cent. The greatest difference in employee communication between the UK and other European countries, however, do not occur in individual but in collective employee communication.

## COLLECTIVE CHANNELS OF COMMUNICATION

Much of the discussion about employee communication in the late 1980s and early 1990s was about the fate of collective channels of communication such as trade unions or staff consultative committees. The Cranet Survey, in line with other research, confirms that collective channels have not been part of the communication explosion; at the same time the large majority of organizations continue to make some use of collective channels. In practice, where management used to first inform trade unions about proposed changes and new initiatives, this is now more likely to take place parallel to, if not after, direct employee communication fora have been used.

During the decade there has been a small but steady move away from collective communication, somewhat more so for upward than downward communication. A fifth of organizations do not use trade unions in downward communication, nor do a quarter for upwards communication. (*see* Tables 7.5 and 7.7). For the first half of the 1990s the share of organizations moving away from representative communication clearly exceeded those moving to expand it. This changed in the last round of the research (*see* Table 7.5). The change has not been dramatic but confirms other trends that union influence and union membership have stabilized, and in some sectors might be building strength. While there has been little legislation forcing organizations to consult with trade unions (and at the time of the survey the Employee Relations Act (1999) and its regulations concerning trade union recognition would not have had an impact), since the election of the Labour Government in 1997 there clearly has been a greater emphasis on social partnership at work.

| | UK 1991 | 1992 | 1995 | 1999 | EU 1999 |
|---|---|---|---|---|---|
| Increase | 16 | 12 | 12 | 18 | 22 |
| Decrease | 21 | 19 | 16 | 9 | 6 |
| Not used | * | * | 17 | 20 | 8 |

* Data not available

**TABLE 7.5**

**Change in the use of collective channels for downward communications (in % of organizations)**

| | UK 1999 Manufacturing | Other industry | Business services | Other services | Public sector |
|---|---|---|---|---|---|
| Increase | 22 | 13 | 9 | 16 | 25 |
| Decrease | 14 | 11 | 6 | 9 | 9 |
| Not used | 18 | 33 | 62 | 33 | 2 |

**TABLE 7.6**

**Change in the use of collective channels for downward communications by sector (in % of organizations)**

| | UK 1992 | 1995 | 1999 | EU 1999 |
|---|---|---|---|---|
| Increase | * | 11 | 14 | 19 |
| Decrease | * | 16 | 13 | 11 |
| Not used | 16 | 20 | 24 | 7 |

* Data not available

**TABLE 7.7**

**Change in the use of collective channels for upward communications (in % of organizations)**

| | UK 1999 Manufacturing | Other industry | Business services | Other services | Public sector |
|---|---|---|---|---|---|
| Increase | 15 | 22 | 3 | 13 | 18 |
| Decrease | 19 | 12 | 9 | 11 | 14 |
| Not used | 18 | 33 | 65 | 35 | 1 |

**TABLE 7.8**

**Change in the use of collective channels for upward communications by sector (in % of organizations)**

The scope and nature of collective employee communications clearly depend on business sector. In the finance and business services sector, 62 per cent of organizations report that they do not use collective channels in downward communication, and 65 per cent that they do not use collective channels in upward communication – proportionately twice as many organizations as in any other sector (*see* Tables 7.6 and 7.8). In terms of employee relations this sector is, of course, a somewhat curious mixture between the retail banking sector with well-established collective bargaining procedures, and the finance and business services sector with a high level of non-union organizations. At the other end of the spectrum, virtually all public-sector employers use collective channels. However, all sectors, whether they have high or low levels of collective communication, have seen relatively modest growth in representative employee communication.

The survey also asked directly whether organizations have joint consultative committees or works councils. Slightly under two thirds of organizations operate these, and, as is also confirmed by the 1998 Workplace Employee Relations Survey, the incidence of joint consultative committees increases in line with employee numbers and trade union membership (Cully *et al*, 1999). Once again there is a strong sector effect (*see* Table 7.9).

**TABLE 7.9**

**Organizations with joint consultative committees or works councils by sector (in %)**

| UK 1999 Manufacturing | Other industry | Business services | Other services | Public sector | UK average | EU 1999 EU average |
|---|---|---|---|---|---|---|
| 63 | 49 | 28 | 49 | 94 | 63 | 84 |

## European comparisons

Collective channels of employee communication are considerably more established elsewhere in Europe though the types of arrangements in place vary dramatically. In some countries trade unions play the major role in collective employee relations, in others there are statutory arrangements that are formally independent of trade unions. The incidence of highly unionized organizations, where at least 75 per cent of employees are unionized, varies from over seven out of ten in Finland and Sweden to less than 2 per cent in France and Spain. In France, for example, actual trade union membership is very low but trade unions have the right, irrespective of membership, to demand consultation and information from the employer about a considerable range of internal affairs. Germany, the Netherlands and Austria have formal works-council systems, which, irrespective of trade unions, put obligations for consultation – and participation – on the employer. In the Nordic countries, systems for participation are often less bureaucratic, but the principles of social partnership are firmly enshrined in both social values and company practice; the role of unions in social security administration, moreover, provides continued institutional support for high levels of union membership. Nevertheless, whatever the national framework, some form of collective employee communication channel is provided for.

European employers are considerably less likely to do without collective channels of communication. Three times as many British as European employers do without collective channels of communication (*see* Tables 7.5 and 7.7). Continental employers are also considerably more likely to have works councils or joint consultative committees (*see* Table 7.9). With the exception of Greece, Ireland, Italy and Portugal, nine out of ten organizations have a works council or joint consultative committee. Particularly in Austria, Germany and the Netherlands the extensive rights of works councils make the maintenance of good relations with the works council an important success factor for the human resource management function. Still, even though collective employee representation is far better established in continental Europe than in the UK, trends in the volume of communication are not that different. In most countries, as in the UK, channels of individual communication have seen more growth than collective channels of communication.

## STRATEGIC AND FINANCIAL INFORMATION – THE COMMUNICATION HIERARCHY

The Cranet research clearly shows an increase in employee communication, particularly from management to the workforce. But apart from the use of different channels of communication, what about the actual content? One of the reasons for increased communication is the increased rate of restructuring and the need to focus employees on the business performance of the organization. Hence we examined whether organizations regularly brief the workforce about strategic issues and financial performance. Much

*"Access to information continues to be very hierarchical: less information is provided at the lower levels of the shop floor"*

of recent organizational change has been aimed at making organizations flatter and less hierarchical, giving all employees a sense of involvement instead of making involvement depend on grades and hierarchies. Our research suggests that information flow on strategic and financial issues has become more inclusive during the last decade. Yet access to such information continues to be very hierarchical: less information is provided at the lower levels of the shop floor. Manual workers are not briefed about strategy in almost two thirds of organizations; financial information is provided slightly more widely but still leaves out manual workers in slightly under half of organizations. Clerical and administrative workers do only slightly better, and professional and technical employees are not regularly briefed by a third of employers. Indeed, in the view at least of the human resources directors, even managers cannot be sure to have access to such information in all organizations (*see* Tables 7.10 and 7.11). There has been a clear improvement in the provision of information at lower levels since the early 1990s, but the basic hierarchical features remain. In 1999 slightly under a third of UK organizations report that they regularly brief all employee groups about both financial and strategic issues, compared to slightly over a fifth in 1992.

**TABLE 7.10**

**Organizations regularly briefing employees about strategic issues (in %)**

| | UK 1992 | 1995 | 1999 | EU 1999 |
|---|---|---|---|---|
| Management | 91 | 95 | 94 | 94 |
| Professional/technical | 59 | 72 | 66 | 54 |
| Clerical | 33 | 49 | 46 | 33 |
| Manual | 28 | 41 | 37 | 25 |

**TABLE 7.11**

**The provision of strategic information by sector (in % of organizations)**

| | UK 1999 Manufacturing | Other industry | Business services | Other services | Public sector |
|---|---|---|---|---|---|
| Management | 94 | 98 | 99 | 92 | 96 |
| Professional/technical | 60 | 67 | 72 | 59 | 72 |
| Clerical | 42 | 40 | 52 | 44 | 43 |
| Manual | 40 | 33 | 23 | 38 | 43 |

| | UK | | | EU |
|---|---|---|---|---|
| | 1992 | 1995 | 1999 | 1999 |
| Management | 89 | 95 | 94 | 92 |
| Professional/technical | 70 | 78 | 79 | 73 |
| Clerical | 53 | 61 | 66 | 57 |
| Manual | 48 | 52 | 55 | 43 |

**TABLE 7.12**

**Organizations regularly briefing employees about financial performance (in %)**

| | UK 1999 Manufacturing | Other industry | Business services | Other services | Public sector |
|---|---|---|---|---|---|
| Management | 94 | 98 | 99 | 92 | 92 |
| Professional/technical | 85 | 80 | 82 | 76 | 69 |
| Clerical | 79 | 67 | 67 | 64 | 52 |
| Manual | 71 | 58 | 28 | 58 | 43 |

**TABLE 7.13**

**The provision of information on financial performance by sector (in % of organizations)**

There are considerable differences between sectors (*see* Tables 7.11 and 7.13). Given the rather marginal level of employment of manual workers in most business-service organizations, the low level of their inclusion is perhaps not surprising; otherwise financial and business-service employers are doing comparatively well. The same cannot be said about public services. The pressures on contracting out, market testing, best value and, more generally, improvements in quality and productivity have left few public-sector organizations untouched. At least initially such initiatives were mainly targeted at services that employed a high share of manual workers, so the lack of inclusion of manual workers is more surprising. Within the public sector local government in particular is performing badly. The construction industry is another sector with a high share of manual workers and a poor performance in including them in corporate communication. Manufacturing employers, on the other hand, seem to have taken the messages about inclusive communication more seriously, particularly regarding financial information.

However, the overriding factor explaining whether organizations are likely to share corporate information with employees is not sector but trade union presence. Highly unionized organizations are more than twice as likely as non-unionized organizations to include all employee groups in strategic and financial information. This suggests clearly that collective and individual forms of employee communication are not substitutes but complement each other; and that some collective pressures for communication help to ensure that employers are systematic in workforce communication.

## European comparisons

Perhaps most interesting in terms of international comparisons is whether British employee communication is more or less inclusive than continental systems. On the face of it at least British workforces are more likely to be given corporate information than their European brethren. European manual workers in particular are much more likely to be left out of communication than in the UK (*see* Tables 7.10 and 7.12). Before discussing the implications of this, however, it should be emphasized that the European average comprises diverse national practices. Organizations in the Nordic countries are much more likely than British – or indeed any other – organizations to have inclusive employee communication systems. At the other extreme are Mediterranean countries, including France, where communication practices seem to be particularly hierarchical. Surprisingly perhaps, the countries with the most extensive legislation or statutes on information, consultation and participation – the middle European countries with strong works-council legislation – are less confident that this system delivers strategic information to all employees.

Clearly, in a broad study such as this it is not possible to evaluate the actual delivery of the systems of employee communication. It was left to managerial respondents to define 'formal briefings on strategy or financial performance', and of course we do not know whether employees would actually agree with the managerial responses. As with all international surveys, there is a further factor to take into account when interpreting national responses: cultural differences in the levels of caution or enthusiasm in responses. For example, given that over 90 per cent of German organizations (those with works councils) by law have to hold annual meetings for the whole workforce where senior managers give information about corporate performance and answer employee questions, one would expect human resource directors to report that all employees are formally and regularly briefed. The fact that many of them do not implies something about standards and definitions, in the sense of: we are doing something but should do better – hence we tick 'no'. British employers are much more confident that they provide strategic information. At least in the debates about the extension of employee rights to participation and consultation, British employers tend to argue that they provide the type of information employees actually want: directly relevant to the job and to the individual employee. According to them, the majority of employees have little interest in broader corporate issues. Yet in the continental European view of employee communication, such a lack of interest among many employees is, if anything, an argument for formalized representative rights to consultation and information.

In relation to financial information personnel directors cite a further problem – the restraints put on sharing sensitive information that could influence share values and might lay the organization open to potential accusations of insider trading. This is the subject of a current case in the European courts: MSF (the union for manufacturing, science and finance employees) is taking the British government to court over the need for stronger employee rights to financial information in the case of collective redundancies and take-overs. Perhaps the one clear message is that individual and collective employee communication need to be seen as complementary, and that they are mutually strengthening and reinforcing.

## CONCLUSION

Employee communication has been subject to considerable changes during the last decade. Communication processes used to be more formalized and located firmly in the domain of organized employee relations. The last decade has seen a continuation in the dramatic decline in the role of trade unions within organizations and a change on the employers' part from centralized communication through personnel departments to greatly increased – and hence more diffused – communication by line managers. Thus the role of personnel departments is changing from being a channel of communication to facilitating effective direct communication between line managers and their teams. The explosion in direct communication – be it through new technology, be it by reinforcing the role of line managers – places greater responsibility on managers to co-ordinate increasingly diverse communication channels. The survey results suggest that in relation to corporate strategic and financial information employee communication systems are either not performing well or that this is not an issue of strategic importance for organizations.

*"The explosion in direct communication places greater responsibility on managers to co-ordinate increasingly diverse communication channels"*

European comparisons suggest that in the absence of extensive statute on employee information and consultation, UK employers are more active in exploring individual channels for employee communication, and that, at least in the assessment of UK human resource directors, British employee communication practices compared to those in many other European countries are more inclusive of all employee groups. Yet British and European unions argue that individual employee communication is not a substitute for representative employee communication; and that it takes expertise and specialization to be an active recipient of corporate information. Employee involvement for them requires both an individual and collective dimension to be truly effective. It is likely that the issue of employee communication, particularly of a strategic nature, will remain on the European agenda for the considerable future.

## REFERENCES

Cully, M., Woodland, S., O'Reilly, A. & Dix, A. (1999) *Britain at Work: As depicted by the 1998 Workplace Employee Relations Survey*. London: Routledge.